IS THERE
AN ANSWER
TO
DEATH ?

SPECTRUM BOOKS IN HUMANISTIC PSYCHOLOGY,

edited by Rollo May and Charles Hampden-Turner, aim to present those psychological viewpoints that place the human being at the organizing center of social reality. It assumes that persons have potential for growth and unfolding in relationship with others, that the ideas they hold about themselves have important consequences, at least partly self-fulfilling. Human beings are free to choose, yet choices once made have determinable, and sometimes inexorable, results, for which the social scientist must share responsibility. In short, we posit an unbreakable relationship between the knower and the known to which each contributes.

We present this series in the hope that a science of the human being will evolve which is worthy of the humanistic tradition and the richness of human endowments.

Rollo May

Charles Hampden-Turner

General Editors

PETER KOESTENBAUM is Professor of Philosophy at San José State University. He has received the statewide Outstanding Professor Award of the California State University and Colleges. His other books include *Managing Anxiety: The Power of Knowing Who You Are*, *Existential Sexuality: Choosing to Love*, and *The Vitality of Death: Essays in Existential Psychology and Philosophy*.

PETER KOESTENBAUM

IS THERE
AN ANSWER
TO
DEATH?

PRENTICE-HALL, INC., *Englewood Cliffs, New Jersey*

Library of Congress Cataloging in Publication Data

Koestenbaum, Peter (date).
    Is there an answer to death?

    (Spectrum Books in humanistic psychology) (A
Spectrum Book)
    Includes bibliographical references and index.
    1. Death.   I. Title.
BD444.K64   128'.5   76–1939
ISBN 0–13–506105–9
ISBN 0–13–506097–4 pbk.

Special thanks are due to the series editors and to Michael Hunter, Jean Homan, and Martha Culley, as well as to Peggy Granger, Mary Allen, and Norma Karlin for their skillful help in the preparation of this book.

10 9 8 7 6 5 4 3

Prentice-Hall International, Inc., *London*
Prentice-Hall of Australia Pty. Limited, *Sydney*
Prentice-Hall of Canada, Ltd., *Toronto*
Prentice-Hall of India Private Limited, *New Delhi*
Prentice-Hall of Japan, Inc., *Tokyo*
Prentice-Hall of Southeast Asia Pte. Ltd., *Singapore*

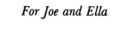

For Joe and Ella

Contents

PART THREE
CONSCIOUSNESS AND THE INDIVIDUAL

PART FOUR
IMMORTALITY AND THE INDIVIDUAL

Introduction

DYING

It was an unusual party to say the least. It is rare enough when any kind of party is held in a hospital. But when the hostess is a cheery-voiced terminal cancer patient who is throwing her own "going away party," the designation of party moves from rare to unique.

Coffee and cookies were served to friends and relatives alike while the hostess looked on approvingly from her bed. She graciously accepted flowers, telegrams, and telephone calls from all over the country while scores signed the guest register. There was much chatter and laughter.

"Everyone says I look better," she told a young guest. "Do you know why?" She pointed one finger over her head. "I have a date up there with God. Today is my happy day." In truth, the hostess was not even sure she would last until the next day.

"Demonstrated proof," said one reporter covering the story, "that even death can be happy and beautiful."

The depth of the coverage of the party in the San Francisco Bay Area newspapers gave ample evidence that this was more than a feature story about a brave and gallant woman. Her attitude toward death was so rare that her party was actually *news*.

Two months later and contrary to all expectations, she was still alive and strong. Could it be that facing death significantly enhanced her physical and emotional strength to live? We shall explore the philosophic grounds for her health.

The point is that we all realize that death is inevitable, yet no one wants to talk about it, face it, or do anything about it. It is a subject

1

that is locked in a closet or tucked away in a dark corner. The feeling is that it is there, all right, but let's not acknowledge it.

The intention of this book is to take death out of its hiding place and confront it. But by no means will this be a morbid or depressing book. Quite the reverse. I want to show you how the analysis of death fits into the picture of life; that there is an existential theme on death and there are appropriate times in the life of an individual when the notion of dying can bring a greater meaning to his life.

Further, it is my hope that you will see that by focusing and understanding the inevitability of your death you will be afforded comfort and surcease in an area that all too frequently means only suffering, fear, and pain.

A second, equally basic theme will be that of consciousness. "Consciousness" is one of the obvious existential answers to the question "Who am I?", which will be a continuing topic throughout this book. Understanding consciousness may be the answer to death.

And this brings us to a final introductory word. I am a professor of philosophy and have been for many years. Naturally my approach to these questions will be a philosophical one. But that is not to say that we will be dealing with abstruse, difficult concepts. Just as I try to do in my classes, I intend to be as practical in the following pages as I possibly can. We all participate in the suffering of mankind, and we should think it a privilege to help enlist philosophy into the service of the needs of our fellow human beings. We all need compassion. Always the reader will get direct, applicable, and practical answers when he asks, "But what does this mean to *me*? How is this going to affect *my* life? Why should I *care* about facing something as scary and unpleasant as my own death?"

I ask only that you read on. Through experience, example, and exercises, it is my hope that together we will discover the meaning and value of a positive confrontation with death, and, also together, perhaps find an answer.

PURPOSE

In this book I hope to give help to those who are anxious about death. But its purpose is also larger than that: it seeks to fulfill an important theoretical task as well.

This book is my third contribution to help establish the philosophic approach to mental health as a bona fide science, academic discipline, and profession. Three interchangeable titles for this new field of study and new professional specialty describe best the function of philosphy for the future of human fulfillment and happiness: We can refer to these books as covering the topic of "philosophy and health," "existential psychotherapy," or "humanistic psychotherapy." I prefer to call this new discipline "personalized education in philosophy."

A principal underlying assumption of personalized education in philosophy is that many, including the most important, issues in psychotherapy are philosophical rather than psychological or medical. Although much has been said, practiced, and written about the interconnections between philosophy and psychotherapy, there are two major problems with that material. First, most of it is written by professional therapists, many of whom have only limited knowledge of philosophy. To understand philosophy requires the same kind of practice and experience that a therapist needs: thousands of hours of practicum work to learn what happens when one's concepts are put into practice. Second, this connection has never been presented systematically and explored from a philosophic point of view. What we miss is a general theory; what we lack is to show how the marriage of philosophy and health is the logical outgrowth of the history of world philosophy.

To help perform these tasks is the purpose of my books.

The two books published so far contain a detailed presentation of what I call the existential personality theory, with references to both its theoretical foundations and its therapeutic applications. That matter is discussed in Part One of *Managing Anxiety*,[1] which is the first book. Published also is a general analysis of the *negative* (the empty) aspects of existence, such as anxiety, suffering, guilt, and the like. That theme is covered in Part Two of *Managing Anxiety*. A third theme is the analysis of the *positive* (the solid and substantial) in human existence, in particular love and the general phenomena of encounter and intersubjectivity. These matters are developed in detail in my second book, *Existential Sexuality*.[2] This book develops with greater specificity the theme of death—which is one of the dominant negative aspects of life. Although it is best to read these books in sequence, each can be understood on its own and can be profitably read independently.

---

[1] Englewood Cliffs, N.J.: Prentice-Hall, 1974.
[2] Englewood Cliffs, N.J.· Prentice-Hall, 1974.

PART ONE

OVERVIEW

1

The Two Revelations
of Death

THE INDIVIDUAL AND THE COSMIC

The current interest in death originated with the existentialist philosophers, especially Kierkegaard and Nietzsche, with the novelists Dostoevski and Tolstoy, and with their followers Heidegger and Sartre. The topic has been taken over by psychologists. The basic philosophical point made in the study of death is this: Death is not an experience but either a felt anticipation or a sorrowful loss. In any event, death is an influential self-concept. And it is this certainty about our eventual death and that of all other human beings that is the key to understanding our human nature. Let me be specific. Death—our own and that of others—explains what it means to be human (searching for meaning, immortality, freedom, love, and individuality) far better than the psychological principles of sex and aggression, the biological instincts of survival and procreation, the utilitarian theories of happiness and approbation, or the religious ukase of God's will.

The anticipation of our death reveals to us who we are. It is an *intellectual* revelation, in that death helps us define human nature. But it is also an *experiential* understanding, in that death puts us in touch with our deepest feelings—both anxieties and hopes, both needs and opportunities—as existent human beings.

Two Worlds

Of particular importance is the fact that death reveals us to ourselves as participating in two worlds: the universal and the particular.

7

Only death (not sex or survival) reveals that the person has a unique place in being, a place not occupied by any other creature in the universe. Thus, death reveals us as part human and part divine, as part person and as part God.

Death reveals us as being *both* individual *and* cosmic; it demonstrates that we participate in both a temporal and an eternal realm. Death shows us up as both fragile and indestructible. In the technical language of phenomenology, man has an empirical as well as a transcendental dimension. And it is the business of the professional philosopher to develop the profound significance which that bipolarity has for the lives of individual human beings.

Philosophy must come to our aid in moments of need. The questions surrounding death—how to adapt ourselves to it, how to manage it, and how, perhaps, to overcome it—demand answers for you and for me. We, as the human race, must search for them collectively.

The present book may be one of the few that gives adequate consideration to *both* of these apparently contradictory revealing aspects of death. Atheistic existentialism—often associated with Nietzsche, Sartre, and Camus—restricts itself to exploring human beings as finite. Theistic existentialism, on the other hand, explores human nature as infinite. Existential philosophers associated with the exploration of our possibilities for infinity (sometimes also called "participation" or "encompassing") include such figures as Marcel, Jaspers, and perhaps Kierkegaard, Tillich, Buber, Maritain, and Berdyaev. In this book I hope to explore in detail how we *choose* ourselves as either individual or as cosmic and develop the significance of that choice for our daily problems, including issues that are often called psychological.

Human beings participate in two worlds. We are neither physical objects exclusively nor are we spiritual or conscious entities alone. We live out our lives on the interface between the two. This point has been stated emphatically, clearly, and centrally in two influential existential personality theories: that of Heidegger in *Being and Time* and especially in that of Sartre in his *Being and Nothingness.* The struggle and stress, the tension and excitement that exist in the persistent interaction, love, and collision of these two worlds make up the history of our human existence. Human problems—love and anxiety, success and failure, acceptance and rejection, pain and illness, pleasure and deprivation, poverty and oppression, revolution and war, crime and injustice, and so forth—occur on the level of this interface and must be resolved with our full and accepting understanding of this interface. The world today shows gross ignorance of this ancient philosophic insight and exhibits unconscionable neglect in its application.

Examples

Let us consider two examples. Political problems are handled today by manipulation—either through attempts to establish a Metternich-like balance of power, as in the area of foreign policy, or by pushing the buttons of the economic machine, such as the Federal Reserve Bank's control of the money supply—while ignoring the concurrent and equally important spiritual or philosophical causes altogether. Lifestyles and world views as well as conceptions of the nature of the person and his values—phenomena that exist in the world order of consciousness or subjectivity rather than in that of matter or objectivity—have as much influence in world affairs as do physical causes. In politics we need not only manipulators; we also need inspired and humane, visionary and compassionate leaders. We are a world of materialists. Our problems will never be resolved until we move from this viewpoint to one that recognizes that human beings participate in *two* world orders.

Another example of our failure to apply these philosophic insights is found in the licensing of healers. I fully recognize the superficial reasons for and advantages of licensing anyone, especially healers, and I do not propose any facile, irresponsible, and simplistic solutions. But behind the specific application of that practice lies a fundamental materialistic, one-world-order prejudice (I call it the "ghost-in-a-machine" theory of personality): that human problems exist only in the order of the material world (which includes the body with all its feelings and emotions). The bona fide healers are biologists—sitting on the board of medical examiners—or experimentalists and statisticians (to oversimplify a situation) sitting on the board for the behavioral sciences (rather than *human* sciences, *spiritual* sciences, or the sciences of *consciousness*—which happens to be the original meaning of the words "psychology" and "psychiatry"). Marital problems, for example, are not considered dysfunctions in the area of a philosophy of life, but are treated by the teaching of skills that will cause behavior changes and emotional reconditioning. That may be an oversimplification. But I believe that the theoretical outlines are correct.

The implication is—and it is not merely a matter of philosophical opinion protected by the First Amendment to the Constitution but is written into law and is thus a philosophical posture mandated by the State—that the "correct" theory of personality is a materialistic, object-centered philosophy. Interface or dialectical theories, which I call field-of-consciousness personality theories, are, in practice, illegal. And because I feel the latter to be true, I consider this state of affairs tragic for the well-being of mankind. The State has entered the field of philosophy and ruled on the truth. That indeed sounds totalitarian and dictatorial. I worry but have no easy practical solutions. There are no individual culprits in this situation. We are all victimized, in the words of Santayana, by "winds of doctrine" blowing from the land of philosophic naivete and ignorance.

Let us now proceed to a brief overview of the two dialectically opposed revelations about our possibilities as human beings, potentialities that are open to those persons who confront the inevitable reality of death. These are the persons who allow Death to speak and are willing to hear his words.

INDIVIDUALITY

First, consider how death reveals man as individual and concrete. Dostoevski writes, in *The Idiot*, what is in fact an autobiographical statement:

> This man had once been led out with the others to the scaffold and a sentence of death was read over him. . . .   Twenty minutes later a reprieve was read to them, and they were condemned to another punishment instead. Yet the interval between those two sentences, twenty minutes or at least a quarter of an hour, he passed in the fullest conviction that he would die in a few minutes. . . .   The The priest went to each in turn with a cross. He had only five minutes more to live. He told me that those five minutes seemed to him an infinite time, a vast wealth. . . .   But But he said that nothing was so dreadful at that time as the continual thought, "What if I were not to die! What if I could go back to life—what eternity! And it would all be mine! I would turn every minute into an age; I would lose nothing, I would count every minute as it passed, I would not waste one!" He said that this idea turned to such a fury at last that he longed to be shot quickly.[1]

Confronting one's own death, facing up to it, owning up to it, accepting it, integrating it fully into one's experience—all of these psychological realities give us the fullness and richness of the experience of life. The tragic and unfortunate circumstances of death nevertheless give us—vicariously for those who do not confront their own death but only read how others do it—a genuine appreciation for the beauty and the sanctity of life.

Psychotherapy needs this philosophical insight, because much of the

[1] Quoted in William Barrett, *Irrational Man* (New York: Anchor Books, 1962), p. 140.

therapeutic process consists in helping the patient fulfill his destiny, not as a participant in the flow of the cosmic spirit (unless the therapeutic emphasis is transpersonal), but as a unique, isolated, and finite individual. I have coined the expression "To be human means to freely choose one's finitude." It focuses the issue of being an individual and of taking responsibility for being such.

Much of the material in this book develops the idea of what for lack of better language might be called atheistic or conventional existentialism. Some of the central and individualistic themes that thus emerge are the following:

1. We need death in order to savor life.
2. Death is an "invention" needed and therefore created for the sake of feeling alive.
3. Death puts us in touch with the sense of a real, individual existence.
4. Death makes possible decisions for authenticity—that is, courage and integrity.
5. Death gives us the strength to make major decisions.
6. Death reveals the importance of intimacy in life.
7. Death helps us ascribe meaning of our life retroactively, a useful concept for older people.
8. Death shows us the importance of ego-transcending achievements.
9. Death shows us the path to self-esteem. It gives us the capacity to do something important.

Death reveals me as an individual. Specifically and in detail, what are the consequences of this insight for daily living? As I have written in *The Vitality of Death*,[2] death reveals me as finite:

1. Man cannot escape death. He must construct his life with the clear realization of that fact. He must accept the fact that he has been condemned to death. Then *he can start living.* He will then *neutralize fear.*
2. Once he has recognized death, the individual is on the way to becoming *decisive*.
3. By remembering death, man concentrates on *esssentials*.
4. Through the awareness of death an individual achieves *integrity*.
5. The person who knows he will die *finds meaning* in life.
6. Death makes man *honest.*
7. The realization of death leads to *strength*.
8. To accept death means to *take charge* of one's life.
9. The thought of death helps one to assume a *total plan for life.*
10. Awareness of death *breaks the stranglehold of failure.*

[2] Westport, Conn.: Greenwood Publishers, 1971.

ETERNITY

But death can also reveal the eternal in the person; it can reveal us as spiritual and transpersonal beings. This revelation of death is precisely the opposite of the above. And I make no value judgments. Both revelations of death are real. The conflict between the two is a defining characteristic of our being-in-the-world. Death can help us realize that overcoming our sense of finitude, that realizing the eternal nature of our solitary and silent center, can also be the meaning of life. This revelation of the meaning of death is a second-tier answer to the problem of death.

The truth of this concept of the eternal in us can be accentuated by reflecting on some of its consequences.

1. An extraordinary *relaxation of anxiety.* The creation of time and finitude bring about the anxiety of deadlines and accomplishments as well as the anguish of irremediable loss. That this should be the case will be discussed later in the book. With the discovery of the dimension of the eternal in us, a great peace descends over our existence.

2. A major *release of* living and creative *energy.* The *decision for finitude*—which is a central concept in this existential personality theory—is the decision for blocking, damming up, repressing, boxing in, restricting, tightening up, stiffening—that is, alienating, separating, and thus individualizing ourselves. When the possibility of undercutting or reversing this decision is finally recognized, two events take place. First, the "natural" energy, libido or life force is released. The dam's floodgates open and the water rushes out smoothly and without impediments. Second, the energy and focusing involved in the decision for finitude, individualization, and no-saying is now redirected into yes-saying. I must add that the term "energy" is a phenomenological one, which means that it is a metaphor meant to elicit the perception of the flow that is the field of consciousness or our being-in-the-world.

3. A delightful *surge of freedom.* Great as the decision for being a finite human may be, it has in it elements of prison, shackling, and self-denial. Understanding the Eternal Now can be the experience of setting us free. That understanding gives us the sense of freedom, symbolized in the high-flying bird, for which modern man so desperately craves.

4. The final consequence follows from *integrating* the experience of immortality in a finite life. This integration of the two contradictory revelations of death is an act of artistic balance. It is a redefinition of

our finitude. It is achieving a sense of wholeness. Before the insight of lived immortality, the individual may sometimes see himself as a slave. He often feels miserable and he is crushed with the weight of worries. After the insight that the two opposing dialectical poles can be integrated into one whole life he is a free person and an aristocrat in living. He knows how to live well and has overcome his earlier compulsions to worry. His body, his social environment, and the physical world in which he lives will then reflect this wholesome integration of his finitude with the eternal in him.

Understanding the meaning of death is the beginning of all philosophic wisdom.

2

Theoretical Foundations

POLARITY

This is not a technical book, meant only for the specialist. However, for those who are interested in the question of theoretical foundations, it is important at the outset to give a clear idea of the philosophical argument and psychological purpose of this book. Our knowledge of the experience of death is either our participation in the real or expected death of another person or it is the anticipation of our own. This book discusses how to come to terms with death, not in the sense of coping or adjusting, but in what I believe to be the more important sense of uncovering deeper philosophic truths.

Process

The background of my position is the dialectical or polar nature of existence, as we have discussed in Chapter 1. Existence is process and not object. Few take that point seriously. We often verbalize that we are not things or objects, but in practice we exhibit much suffering that can be traced directly to our unconscious conviction that we *are* things. Many ordinary problems of living resolve themselves when we understand that we are in fact *process.*

Existence is rich in contradictions and stresses. In fact, the tensions in life brought about by "the two hands of God" constitute the excitement that is the actual experience of being alive. Optimum stress is both the joy and anxiety of existing; it brings about the experience of energy and potency. The stress of our polarization is also the experi-

14

ence of being grounded: we find a home; we discover our foundation.

But there are limits to stress. Excessive excitation is as deadening as insufficient stress.

Perhaps the most significant polarity of life is brought about by the two revelations of death: the finitude of human existence on the one hand and its infinity on the other. This book covers both. We need not opt for either, but we must underscore the dialectical tension between them. We must be sensitive to existential individualism to the same extent that we should appreciate the Eastern philosophies of the detached consciousness. All great philosophies have made contributions to our understanding of existence and we might prefer not to choose one over another but rather discover how conflicting views complement each other in one broader picture. As in a large family, the world philosophies form one system.

We must avoid reductionism. We cannot argue, as some behavioral scientists might, that the consciousness that has withdrawn itself from the world is autistic or catatonic. That interpretation sets up the *finite* possibility of existence as absolute, as the standard, as the final truth. The evidence of direct and presuppositionless experience does not permit such a one-sided theory, one which, in my opinion, is instead the result of a decision (or of what I call an archetypal choice) about our basic world view. Nor can we maintain, as some yogis might, that the truth about existence is a detached, impersonal, and timeless consciousness and that all worldly phenomena are but the illusions of Maya. That is another form of unacceptable reductionism, because it is an interpretation that sets up the impersonal and infinite consciousness as the standard, the truth, and the final value of existence. Again, a presuppositionless analysis of experience does not support such a monolithic and inflexible conclusion. The truth lies in the eternal stress, polarity, and dialectic between these two possibilities revealed by death. Our final philosophic position may be a maverick one, since we are not obligated to make a commitment to either of today's two dominant world views.

Jung

C. G. Jung has written, in his introduction to *The Secret of the Golden Flower*, that the West must reach the insights of the East through its own tradition. That is what has happened in the phenomenological movement in philosophy. Jung was prophetic. Much of contemporary philosophy is not reductionistic but can accept polarity as ultimate.

And the polarities in question are the East–West polarity and the finite–infinite polarity, the latter having being revealed to us through death. Jung defines the mature individual as one who has reached a stage of life in which he feels whole, in which his need for choosing among polar opposites has been overcome. This person has been able to integrate into his existence the ambiguities and contradictions of life.

The phenomenological movement is one of these contemporary dialectical philosophies whose origins antedate the work of Jung.

PHENOMENOLOGY AND EXISTENTIALISM

Phenomenology is a major philosophic posture encompassing both methodology and ontology. Existentialism is a spinoff from phenomenology. The former results from applying phenomenological research techniques to an exploration of the foundations of human existence. The first-tier impact of the phenomenological movement has been in the exploration of human finitude, a task carried out with brilliant inspiration by such philosophers as Kierkegaard, Nietzsche, Heidegger, Sartre, and Camus. We refer to this activity, technically, as philosophical anthropology or descriptive phenomenology. The founder and developer of phenomenology, Edmund Husserl, emphasized in addition the discipline he called *transcendental* phenomenology. Without knowing it, he had reached the same insights which Buddhism and Hinduism had achieved millennia earlier. Transcendental phenomenology is the analysis of pure consciousness, and this analysis is a product exclusively of the development of 2500 years of Western philosophy. The implications of transcendental phenomenology for life and for psychotherapy are still in the early stages of exploration. In this book, through its development of immortality as one answer to death, I hope to carry on the work of transcendental phenomenology. I consider this direction to be the next development in a complete and burgeoning existential philosophy.

Three important consequences follow from the phenomenological-existential analysis of human existence. First, we can develop a thorough philosophical understanding of the meaning of being an individual. That issue is probably the central one in psychotherapy and it is one whose philosophic underpinnings have not been adequately explored. Second, the transition from one world view to another is connected with the freedom of consciousness, one of the defining characteristics of individuality. As a result, we can meaningfully talk about assuming full, free, and personal responsibility for two crucial aspects of our existence: being an individual and overcoming death. The existential (individualistic) as well as the religious (universalistic) world views can now be recognized to be in effect freely chosen. The last consequence of these views is that there is an answer to death in the sense that we can choose one. I hold that we can choose to be individuals—which gives us existential, social, and political reality—but that we also can choose to participate in the universal or cosmic consciousness (or the Eternal Now) that runs through us, and this is a choice that gives us immortality.

Action and Reflection

Some may wonder that existentialism, which is a philosophy of individualism and action, should also emphasize the importance of pure consciousness, which is a more mystical position. The dependence of existentialist philosophers on the basic insights of phenomenology is made clear by such obvious facts as (1) the dedication of Heidegger's major work, *Being and Time,* one of the central works of existentialism, to Edmund Husserl; and (2) the subtitle of Jean-Paul Sartre's masterwork, *Being and Nothingness,* which is "An Essay on Phenomenological Ontology." Hazel Barnes, the brilliant exponent of Sartre's philosophical position, accentuates this relationship between phenomenology and existentialism—which, in its transcendental dimension, concerns itself with the exploration of pure consciousness—when she writes:

> *Sartre. . . follows Husserl in holding that all consciousness is consciousness of something; that is, consciousness is intentional and directive, pointing to a transcendent object other than itself. . . . Secondly, the pre-reflective cogito is non-personal. It is not true that we can start with some such statement as "I am conscious of the chair." All that we can truthfully say at this beginning stage is that "there is (il y a) consciousness of the chair." The Ego (including both the "I" and the "Me") does not come into existence until the original consciousness has been made the object of reflection. Thus there is never an Ego-consciousness but only consciousness of the Ego. . . .*
> *According to Sartre, the Ego is not in consciousness, which is utterly translucent, but in the world; and like the world it is the object of consciousness. . . . Strictly speaking, we should never say "my consciousness" but rather "consciousness of me."*[1]

This quotation makes clear that human beings are not natural objects—and as such ought not to be studied exclusively through medi-

---

[1] Translated by Hazel E. Barnes (New York: Philosophical Library, 1956), introduction (by Barnes) p. x.

cine and the behavioral sciences—but belong to or are the interface between two intertwined but irreconcilably different worlds: the one of objects and the other of pure consciousness.

3

Philosophy and Health

This book is not only theoretical. It is also a confession. We all need to share our very personal reflections on the subject of death. Death is more than merely an abstraction. We need more than a summary of the theories of others on death. To be an existentialist philosopher means to live one's philosophy. We must make certain that in these reflections on death we do not escape the issue of death—by treating that sensitive topic as if it were a bacterial specimen under a microscope and not a disease gnawing at the very brain that is looking through the microscope. Each of us must, through these pages, face his own death, come to terms with his own death. And I must do this not only for the sake of others, such as my readers, but for my own sake. Only if I come to terms with my own death and have my reader as my witness can I be of assistance in his efforts to come to terms with his.

In discussing such expectations, we will in this chapter discuss the nature of philosophic understanding and how such understanding aids us, as limited human beings, to handle the idea of death. We will begin to see how self-disclosure and authenticity must be a part of any healing process—and how our grasping of the cosmic consciousness relates to concepts of physical and mental well-being, immortality, and death.

WHAT IS AUTHENTICITY?

Authenticity has three components: philosophic understanding, free and subjective problem solving, and avoidance of objective manipulation.

Understanding

The authentic person must have an accurate understanding of his human nature and of his relation to the world. In addition, that understanding must be expressed and integrated in his life.[1] Such a condition of understanding is not limited to therapeutic interventions; it can also be accomplished in a variety of ways: readings, lectures, classes, seminars, workshops, and private instruction. Every person interested in the question of his own authenticity owes it to himself to attempt to understand human nature. Existentialism and phenomenology offer a synthesis of what is usually termed the *growth movement* or what Abraham Maslow called the *third force in psychology*. Included in the ideal total therapeutic program are—in addition to psychological and medical ideas—also philosophic, theological, oriental, artistic, and literary concepts.

Freedom and Subjectivity

The authentic person must recognize that problems concerned with the question of the meaning of life—ignorance of which leads to inauthenticity—must be solved through his own *freedom* and in his own *subjectivity*. The problem of the meaning of life, which includes the issue of coming to terms with death, can be solved only by the individual himself; he cannot have others do it for him.

Here lies one of the resistances against philosophy, which is why it is neither as well known nor as widely used as medicine. Philosophy is difficult and, to make matters worse, it works only when understood. In fact, I would risk saying that the idea of immortality (and/or reincarnation) works and is meaningful only to the extent that its philosophic underpinnings are understood. In other words, immortality is not automatic. Immortality and reincarnation are experiences and also insights into the structure of human existence. *Having* these experiences and *understanding* these insights resolves many of our most distressing problems. Immortality and reincarnation are experiences which we can have if we understand this philosophy properly. They are the experiences of ultimate peace and security. And these experiences are not illusory but based on solid philosophical analysis.

What I am saying is that immortality is available only to those who

---

[1] This point is developed in detail in Part 1 of my *Managing Anxiety* (Englewood Cliffs, N.J.: Prentice-Hall, 1974).

understand the field-of-consciousness theory of man (the position that a pure subjective consciousness goes through me, to be discussed later in this book). This point is expressed in Christianity's view that you must believe to be saved and in the oriental view that understanding these matters releases you from the wheel of samsara. The ultimate reality and the present benefits of the sense of immortality can come only to those who possess necessary philosophic understanding. Philosophic understanding of human nature is the key to authenticity and this understanding cannot be left to the experts. It must be understood to work. Therefore, the leaders and healers of society must have a thorough understanding of a philosophy of personality. Plato was right when he invented the philosopher-king.

Philosophy is a central feature in the total healing process: it should undergird medicine, psychotherapy, and even hospital administration. And religion is not a substitute for philosophy, although many try to make it such. We live in an age in which the literal interpretations of religious solutions—though very much alive (note the many religiously sponsored hospitals and the many directors of pastoral care in them)—no longer have the power and finality they once had, let us say, in medieval Europe. Fortunately for most patients, some of the best philosophers in hospitals are the pastors.

In a manner of speaking, therefore, a philosophic understanding of the structure of human existence functions like medicine, in that ingesting and absorbing it—i.e., understanding it—will make possible the sane clarification necessary to lead us to actions that will resolve many of the personal, social, and political problems afflicting us today. The benefit begins with the philosophical understanding of what it means to exist as a human being in the world, and no meaningful action can be taken without such knowledge. This fact applies in a foremost way to death.

Avoidance of Manipulation

In order to achieve this philosophic understanding we must guard against the manipulative approach to life. One of the most pervasive characteristics of inauthenticity in our culture is that subjective problems are projected onto objective reality. What in actual fact must be solved in the subjective realm is perceived instead as being an objective matter. Love and meaning become objective things attainable through manipulation rather than subjective processes to be managed through our free will. The healing of sickness is judged to be achieved through material means—pills, shots, surgery—with little or no concern for the human, personal conception of pain, mortality, death in relation to physical or mental illness.

Examples are numerous. Reliance on experts is one. Some experts help you help yourself. These are the authentic healers. Others will do it for you. Except in rare exceptions, the latter is a morally fraudulent approach—be it in medicine or therapy, education or marriage, business success or parenthood. We send children who have behavior problems to the "expert"—the counselor or therapist—to heal or cure them, rather than to understand that their problems exist in relationship to us and only with our help can they be solved.

To solve personal problems from within our silent and solitary center can often mean that we see ourselves and the world, in Spinoza's words, "from the aspect of eternity." The prerequisite to solving problems, or discovering their insignificance, is to perceive them accurately in their total context. One common form of escape, a defense against facing the problem of the meaning of life or of death, is to manipulatively project these major subjective philosophic issues onto small irrelevant objects in the world. Thus, the *subjective* matter of managing one's finitude—the question of limits and frustrations, and eventually death—becomes translated into the *objective* problems of, say, sex, or aches and pains. It can be even worse, as when the larger *subjective* philosophic issues are transferred, in the lives of many, to the *objective* problems of laundry and white teeth, chewing gum and shampoo.

There is much money to be made in exploiting this type of inauthenticity—that is, salvation through manipulation. Those who encourage the belief that philosophic problems—which are universal, personal, and subjective—can be solved through manipulation and in terms of projections on things and externalities, and then *sell* them these objects, become rich, immorally. For example, much profound and artistic thinking goes into cigarette and alcohol advertising: Real values are portrayed beautifully. Then the illogical transition is made, through pure association of ideas, that purchase and consumption of the product will bring about the meaningful value (a relation with another human being, communion with nature, contact with one's tradition or unconscious, etc.) so charmingly and imaginatively portrayed.

MEANING, EMBODIMENT, AND IMMORTALITY

The answers to three basic problems are illuminated through an understanding of what I call the *existential personality theory* or the field theory of man: this represents a philosophical approach to psychological questions. These benefits begin with understanding and not manipulation, because there can be no substitute for philosophic insight and understanding.

The problems in question are *meaning, embodiment,* and *immortality.* The solution to the problem of *meaning* is achieved through the acquisition of individuality, direction, and peace of mind. The solution to the problem of *embodiment*[2] demands an understanding of the relationship between the individual and the universe, between man and God; it is to learn to make use of both the divine and the human in ourselves; to fulfill our potential as both a participant in an infinite and cosmic consciousness and an individual chooser in a particular body. Finally, the solution to the problems of *immortality* and death involves a grasp of our freedom, which is our decision-making mechanism. We oscillate between the divine and the human, between the universal and the particular. Herein lies the clue to why we can risk saying that immortality depends on philosophic understanding. Immortality, as one answer to death, is the decision to identify with the universe in us. And that decision can be made only when we are in possession of all the relevant philosophic facts.

Subjectivity and Objectivity

Before turning to details and specifics, we must examine more closely the relation between the subjective and the objective aspects of human experience. Subjectivity is the silent and solitary center. Objectivity is all that is outside that center, that which surrounds it. Objectivity encompasses one's body and feelings, and one's social and physical environment. Our human existence is a *field* which extends from subjectivity to objectivity. We can understand many facets of behavior, individual as well as social, by exploring the interconnections between the subjective and objective poles of that field.

It appears that the principal concern of the age of technology has been the *harnessing of objectivity.* We, as human beings, define ourselves as subjectivities, and we step into the world endeavoring to compensate for this one-sidedness of our nature. In doing so we deny our

---

[2] Embodiment, or its Latinism, incarnation, is the phenomenon of being a body and living the life of the body. The concept is based on the assumption that we are a consciousness-body field and that this consciousness can identify itself with the life of that body or distance itself from it. When consciousness joyously embraces the body's physical demands we say that the person is embodied.

subjective inwardness and invest most of our energies in activities of social manipulation, of which politics is perhaps the best example, and in science and technology.

Inauthenticity

Frequently our concern is not with inner change, which is one way of assuming responsibility for being ourselves, but with a projection of our inward problems onto the world beyond. We then expect to manage the problems of inward meaning vicariously by controlling, dominating, and using our environmont. We do not *accept* our environment—we forcibly modify it. Our concern with harnessing objectivity becomes our measure of worldly success.

Another manifestation of our emphasis on the objective, material world can be found in our body-centeredness: our predilection for spectator sports, the publicity surrounding beauty contests, the popularity of cosmetic surgery, and the obvious and self-conscious psychological importance of our body-image. The pervasive need to conform also illustrates our tendency to work out subjective problems in terms of objective projections. Furthermore, rewards, motivations, and emoluments are not given in terms of self-approval and inner satisfaction, but are instead translated into objective surrogates and numbers. We do not search for meaning but for dollars, not for learning but for grades, not for growth but for approval.

Finally, we think in terms of concrete objects, even if our thinking is about subjectivity. It seems paradoxical that universal inner—i.e., subjective—truths can best be understood through metaphor, example, and pictorial representation. This means we must objectify subjectivity to understand it and to talk about it. These facts about logic and language further illustrate our attempts to reconcile our subjectivity by harnessing objectivity.

Exploitation of nature, of persons, and of societies is made possible by the unethical application of this insight. Deception of the ignorant is made possible by substituting objective gimmicks for inner truths, using for technology the principles of association psychology. Inauthenticity means to do the business of subjectivity through objective surrogates. It means that another person or extraneous object does my living for me.

I do not completely condemn manipulation as a problem-solving device. Authentic problems in the area of harnessing the realm of objectivity involve such matters as the elimination of poverty, crime control, earning money, transportation, communication, physical health, life, protection from weather, etc. However, unless we understand the subjective origins and purposes of these tasks, our efforts are futile. In short, technology must be placed in perspective.

THE BENEFITS OF SELF-DISCLOSURE

Understanding and applying the existential personality theory is the first step towards achieving control over the zone of one's subjectivity. The clarification of such understanding prepares the way for action, which can then produce joy, happiness, a sense of meaning, a justified feeling of importance, reliable self-confidence, and openness for love. Above all, it can answer the problem of death.

Freedom and Energy

Philosophical self-disclosure makes us free. Freedom means an increased sense of personal space and time; it means increased control over one's life and destiny. Freedom means peace of mind and security, self-respect and inner-directedness. It means the release of energy for creative acts and satisfying relationships.

Philosophic understanding is thus a precondition for physical and mental health; obstacles to smooth living can be eliminated. Philosophic understanding can give us the knowledge to act to protect the body and the psyche from the burdens of excessive, unnatural, and irrational (i.e., neurotic) demands.

At the risk of oversimplification, the view can nevertheless be defended that philosophic understanding helps resolve educational, financial, personal, and sexual issues. The individual who has experienced honest philosophical self-disclosure is freed from excessive burdens, including those of distorted self-concepts. The energy thus released can lead to imaginative ideas for progress in one's life. The energy alone will make a difference in the positive direction. In addition, energy and freedom invested in one's imagination are, like brainstorming, paths to promising ideas for successful problem solving.

A key theme is the experience and the concept of "energy." What is the meaning, in philosophical terms, of the rise in energy level? "Energy" as used here is a partially poetic term, one that describes a state of consciousness. Energy is created when the subjective and objective realms of human experience are smoothly integrated. That condition can be deliberately encouraged by using techniques developed in what are known as body therapies and psychosynthesis. The former uses physical exercises and the latter, fantasies; I will go into specific detail about these techniques later on in this text.

Immortality and Reincarnation

We are discussing how philosophical self-disclosure prepares us so that we can take action to better comprehend the zone of subjectivity. I have mentioned joy, freedom, and energy. We must turn to a related insight, one that will give us a clue to better understanding immortality and reincarnation. I believe that what in philosophy are referred to as the a priori sciences—theorems and axioms known to be true without reference to experience or experiment and illustrated by logic, mathematics, geometry, and classical physics—are in fact inextricably bound with the search for subjectivity and consciousness in the individual and in the cosmos. Space and time are in reality the experience of consciousness and subjectivity made "visible." Our personal, individual experience of space and time *is* our experience of the consciousness that flows through us.

I maintain in the spirit of an older philosophy of mathematics and physics that the a priori sciences are in fact *descriptions* of empty space and time, analyses of the *properties* of space and time. The German philosopher Edmund Husserl has coined the word "transcendental" to designate that region of human experience which is the flow of the silent and solitary center, the experience of pure consciousness, a phenomenon called the *atman* in Hinduism. In my opinion, the sciences of space and time are thus one type of description of the consciousness that flows through us, an experience adequately described as *cosmic consciousness.* This hypothesis, just touched upon here, needs to be developed and tested in detail.

One of the important psychological and religious implications of recognizing the cosmic flow within us is that this knowledge enables us to see new possibilities for immortality, reincarnation, and paranormal phenomena. If consciousness is space-time, then eternity (the Eternal Now) and long-distance closeness (the possibility of extrasensory perception) are indeed no mysteries. The only obstacle to merging with the universal is our firm and difficult decision to be individuals. Being an individual is a decision, and it is one that says "no" to that part of the world which is not the individual. The matter of death can be understood and resolved if we understand and integrate into our daily lives these insights about the nature of consciousness. This latter point will be discussed in detail in due time.

Some additional benefits that can follow from philosophically understanding ourselves as a field of consciousness is that this will help us put our lives in order. Philosophic understanding can provide the knowledge, the energy, and the motivation to help us achieve the kind of action and control over life that will enable us to say at the moment of death "my life has been worth living."

Specifically, these insights should also be enlisted to help us develop programs for highly specific problems such as managing addictions, diets, and, in general, facilitate mental and physical health through symptom removal. Philosophic understanding should be used to help us adjust to and cope with disabilities.

In sum and above all, philosophic understanding is meant to give us *hope*.

PART TWO

DEATH
AND
THE INDIVIDUAL

4

The Search for Meaning

The basic theme of Part Two is that it is a better understanding of death that makes us into individuals. This insight facilitates the management of death.

EXISTENTIALISM, THE IDEOLOGY OF THE GROWTH MOVEMENT

The analysis of death is not merely one of many approaches to understanding life—it is the fundamental one. The reason for this contention is that the existential personality theory, for which the anxiety of death is archetypal or primary, is the ideology of the growth movement. Existential philosophy, as part of the phenomenological movement, has the capability of integrating most therapeutic growth approaches into a single system, which is at the same time also a product of the cumulative wisdom of the West.

To fully appreciate the anxiety of death, it would therefore be useful to first consider some approaches to life. In the so-called growth or human potential movement today there is an absolute proliferation of approaches, all with the aim of providing the individual with happiness and the ability to find meaning in life. Some of these approaches are bioenergetics, biofeedback, drugs, encounter groups, family therapy, Gestalt therapy, hypnosis, many types of meditation; as well as paranormal, behavioral, existential and humanistic psychology; additional approaches to human growth are found in the ever-popular Jungian psychology, as well as logotherapy, rational emotive psychology, transpersonal psychology, and psychosynthesis. Finally, many religions, such as Buddhism, Christianity, Hinduism, Islam, Judaism, Sufism, Zen, and yoga, have been enlisted to aid the therapeutic goals of the growth movement.

The vast number of these paths to a better life makes for a very confusing situation. And at this point the reader may well ask what all this has to do with the existential philosophy. Is philosophy just one more confusing addition to an already overcrowded field? Not at all. In fact, existential philosophy puts some order into it. Philosophy gives an overview; it is a synthesizing tool that shows how every one of these new approaches can fit into a larger scheme. *Existential philosophy can be called the ideology of the growth movement.* It provides historical and academic unity.

Put in simplest terms, these individual growth techniques will not answer the basic question upon which philosophy insists: "What is the total plan for your life?" Growth techniques are useful, imaginative, and inspired adjuncts to a basic philosophy of life.

DEATH CONTRIBUTES TO THE TOTAL PLAN FOR LIFE

Death is a philosophical issue, and psychologists did not start talking about its therapeutic importance until the existentialist philosophers pointed out to them that it was important to do so. Existential philosophy focuses on what is central: first, the personal subjective inwardness of man, and second, *consciousness of the world* as the foundation of human values, meanings, and existence.

And this is why I talk about death, and why other existentialists find it extremely important to talk about death. It is because the best way to get the idea, to relate to this notion of a total plan for life, is by confronting your own death. It is such a confrontation that will enable you to demand real and ultimate answers—and to find them!

Your facing of your own death will force you to see your life in a totality, and that includes your future, your present, and that part of your life which is already past. Then you will have to organize and understand that totality. Many people think of death as unreal, as just beyond the horizon, as something they should postpone thinking about—in fact, as an event that is not be mentioned. As a result, they are incapable of experiencing their lives as a whole, of forming any total life plan.

Sole use of any one of the growth approaches mentioned earlier as a means of achieving fulfillment in life is then inherently inauthentic. Exclusive emphasis on techniques and belief in their magical powers is the mark of a technological culture—a culture that substitutes techniques for life, that confuses manipulation of particular objects with the actual process of living, that replaces the mind and the inward consciousness of man with bodies, machines, and tools. It is this belief—that through one particular technique or gimmick you can achieve fulfillment in life—which tragically gives us many of our most serious problems. The truth is, there are no techniques for living. There are techniques for everything else but for living. You are alive, but you must not confuse your aliveness with the techniques that you may use in your search for fulfillment. Only objects respond to techniques. And you are not an object.

What you must realize is that life is right now and right here and living is what you are doing right now. You must attack the problem of living well by *living well.* Substituting technological devices or approaches does not work when it comes to the philosophical issue of living well. Philosophy is not a technique, then, but represents the discovery that techniques are but adjuncts. In short, technological thinking works if you want to build computers or cars or elevators, but it does not work if you want to live. There is no substitute for living; living is *it.*

In his book *The Transformation,* George B. Leonard[1] says that the standard of living—if by that we mean the quality of living—in this country is one of the lowest in the world. Technological devices—cars, refrigerators, etc.—do not seem to lead to a quality of life with which we are really satisfied and of which we can be proud. One only has to look at suburbia—the people who live there have all the nice things that people have always thought they wanted—dishwashers, disposals, yards, space, trees, swimming pools, air conditioning, stereo sets—everything. Yet many of them do not consider themselves happy. They have been misled into believing that instant manipulative solutions are meaningful. And they only find, time and again, that *things* do not bring the kind of "good life" they really want.

DEATH CONTRIBUTES MEANING

Let us return to the idea of death and how confronting it can give meaning to your life. Perhaps I can best explain what I mean by an example that was given me several years ago by a psychiatrist. This psychiatrist had a patient—Nellie B.—who visited him regularly and

[1] New York: Delacorte Press, 1972.

always tried to impress him with her problems. She would say something like, "You didn't think much of my problem last week, but I've *really* got one for your today." His treatment goal was to enable her to change the way she perceived her life: from seeing herself as sick to seeing herself as well, from an attitude of proving absurdity to one of finding meaning.

Unfortunately for this woman, it was not until she developed a fatal disease—uterine cancer—that she acquired the ability to perceive life as a thing of joy rather than of sorrow and self-pity—to realize that her life was good rather than bad. This came from her own confrontation with death.

The fundamental decision of whether life is good or bad comes from an overall view that *you* impose on life. Confronting your own death is one way of arriving at a meaningful conception of life.

Viktor Frankl's *logotherapy* is a useful and related application of the vitality of death. His theory is that human beings are not driven by sex, aggression, or compensation, but by a search for meaning. He believes that people want to find meaning, and when they do, they find a measure of fulfillment. In confronting one's death, Frankl says, we do not necessarily find pleasure, but we do gain a feeling of meaning, substance, and worth that can open us up to experiencing pleasure and joy.[2]

WRITING YOUR OWN OBITUARY

One of the most powerful exercises I could give you at this point to put this discussion on a personal level is to ask you to write your own obituary. In doing this you are actually making a statement of what you have meant in this life when there is no longer anything you can do to change it. You are essentially saying, "This is what I am." Writing out the meaning that your life has had may answer for you the most sensitive question you can ask. You will find that this question is not one of acquiring health, of solving problems; it involves far more than that—it transcends those issues. It is the question of what it

[2] See Viktor E. Frankl, *From Death Camp to Existentialism*, trans. Ilse Lasch, preface by Gordon Allport (Boston: Beacon Press, 1962). See also his *The Will to Meaning: Foundation and Application of Logotherapy* (New York: World Publishing Company, 1969). Frankl's treatise on agony and survival, suffering and death, appeared in his famous book *From Death Camp to Existentialism.* Frankl developed his system of logotherapy during the three years that he was in a concentration camp in Germany during World War II. His contribution consists in expanding one existential truth: in man's most degrading experience it is possible for him to discover his and life's true meaning.

means to be a person, a human being—of how to live well. It is the deepest question of all: what it means to be *you.*

The whole meaning of the burden, the excitement, the terror of living, the responsibility, mystery and holiness of living—all of these meanings emerge clearly when you are forced to confront your own mortality. For even though you never *experience* your death, you are never without the *knowledge* that you *will* die.

There follows a random selection of epitaphs and obituaries, all of which were written by my students in response to my request that they write two obituaries: a real one, which describes them as they actually are, and an ideal one, which describes what they would like to be. Some of these are moving, some are amusing, and all are quite revealing.

OBITUARIES

Actual

Mr. Henry J. A., beloved husband of Mrs. A., father of Michael, John, and Kevin A., dear grandfather of six grandchildren succumbed to an overdose of Red Mountain and barbiturates at 3:30 A.M.

Ideal

At rest and very dead, Henry J. A., former human being, will be missed by the many who knew and cared for him and by the many who knew and didn't like him, and by the many who didn't know him at all. A testament to humanness and hope. Very dead because he was very alive.

WORDS ON A HEADSTONE

Upon my headstone
words will be conceived
by the remaining,
by the bereaved.

They suffer from
a common malady.
They fear to speak
ill of me.

Parents will write,
she was beautiful,
a daughter loving
and dutiful.

Siblings will add,
she was affectionate;
oh, so kind,
we remember her yet.

Friends will say, "sensitive,"
as they shed a tear.
It's a word that's in
this year.

Co-workers will declare
I was idealistic
and displayed admirable
characteristics.

Professors will be quick
when they suggest
I was enthusiastic,
brighter than the rest.

As for myself, should I have
done the choosing,
I would have inscribed
another musing.

She knew life's secret
(the only one worth knowing).
That left her free
to concentrate on growing.

For even as a child
tucked safely in her bed,
she knew that soon, too soon,
she would be dead.

In attempting to write my own obituary, I found that no matter what I wrote, it had no meaning to me whatsoever. What little I had accomplished in the world meant nothing to me simply because my goals themselves became meaningless. Whether I had reached my goals did not seem to make any difference to me for what mattered was that I had goals, that I did not consider my life as something complete. However, in envisioning myself as dead I became nothing more than my past, the sum of all my past actions with no dimension of me projecting itself toward the future. In the face of death, all my hopes, values, loves and my entire past seemed meaningless for I would die alone and for no apparent reason. Death became absolute absurdity and the limiting of freedom. However, this led me to realize that my essence, my meaningful existence is not what I am but rather what I project myself to be. I am a living freedom.

Actual

_____ died today as a result of an automobile accident. Ms. X is survived by her husband and daughters. She was 32 years old. She spent her entire life studying at various schools in preparation for her life. She had hoped to become an anthropologist and had particular interest in the American Indians. She always wanted to donate her time and knowledge for the benefit of these and other oppressed people. Let her memory teach us all that the time to act is upon us.

Ideal

Here lies _____ who died after many years of hard work and devotion to causes of justice and freedom. Ms. X lived and worked with several native American tribes, initially helping to organize peaceful demonstrations calling attention to the needs of our Indian brothers. After this task was completed she continued to donate her time and experience in teaching and writing ethnographies so that the many and varied cultures of the American people would not be lost and would show to each his unique place in the history of man.

Obituary

She fought all her life against the pull of the reins, but though her feet dug deep and the tracks can be seen, she never slowed the stampede.

Obituary for _____

She wondered if anyone ever really knew her. She was light and air—but so often it seemed as if the world saw only a body, a face, behavior.

"Look," she said, "It's me in here—the undefined and undefinable. Hello out there!" (She was given three names and several dozen numbers).

The great comfort of her life was the knowledge that, if she were light and air—evanescent and eternal spirit—then so was everybody else, and maybe some day everyone would understand. . . and everyone would be together.

She watched and waited to see if someone else understood—about the light and air. And now and then, from a glance or a word, it seemed as if someone did understand. She was never quite sure. But perhaps being quite sure was not really necessary. She never stopped searching.

Though she often was no more than a cloudy chunk of quartz, she tried to be—and sometimes was—a prism.

He strived to be good and to understand but he never really got anywhere.

> Here rests Susan—trusting to her friends.
> May her mind lie in peace
> And her spirit roam.

Here I lie, found no meaning, but life was continuously astonishing.

Last night I had a nightmare. Its symbolism was, to my great delight, my coming to grips with the death of myself.

The content of the dream was that I was being embraced by someone from behind. As I attempted to move, I found that I was completely immobilized. All I could do, as my terror rose, was to bite one of the hands, but to no avail. The embrace was not painful but complete.

I woke up at a peak of terror.

When I realized what was happening I immediately comprehended my own fears regarding my own death. I was thankful for the event and in only one other time in my life have I been so moved by my dreams.

My hand is sore from where I had bitten myself.

Shed your tears for those who have lived dying—
Spare your tears for me for I've died living.

Come share a moment of silence.
But shed no tears for this
Child woman
For deep within her soul
She lived in harmony.

Here lies Marc V. who worked hard and steady for 21 years to fill this box.

Success is never final
Failure is never fatal.

She left without a regret or a sorrow
To clutter her heart,
But took with her dreams and hopes
Which never saw their start.

*What Does the Obituary Exercise Teach Us
About the Meaning of Life?*

These obituary writings of the students seemed to fall into several categories, including expression of *guilt about unfulfilled possibilities;* expression of *a need* and demand *for identity and individuality;* discovery of the *importance of intimacy* in life; regret for the lack of *intellectual and artistic development;* and expression of a need for *political achievements* to give meaning to life.

Sorrow over unfulfilled possibilities was expressed by the student who wrote, "Here lies a flower that just started to blossom." Another one wrote, "I am missing so much!"

Another student expressed the theme of his *worthlessness* or lack of importance when he wrote, "R.K.P. died today and it really doesn't make any difference."

Still another category is *immersion in the mystical*. A young man wrote,

> Stone among the stones
> he returned in the joy of his heart
> to the truth of the motionless worlds.

Self-knowledge emerges as an important ideal, as in the case of Jack, who wrote,

> Here lies a man who tried
> To know himself, with only
> Moderate success.

Another common theme is to recognize the importance of *the body* together with its potential for *sensuous pleasures.* Jeff wrote,

> To all here passing by:
> take heed of this tomb and stone,
> for once I lived; now herein lie
> remains of flesh and bone.

He continues,

> . . . *friend of children and wise men, and certain others, lovers of women, the body, art and reason, and the beach, champion of innocence and truth, the capacity for delight and wonder, and dreams; though not without reservations, I was a passionate man.*

Sue expressed *growth*, or process, as the meaning of life discovered through the obituary or epitaph exercise:

> *She created her life. She participated in a profound relationship with another human being. She was a model for others, like herself, who wish to change. She continued the process of human evolution, by educating her children for freedom.*

For Gifford, the discovery about his nature was that *he stands alone.*

> At my death
> All the grand plans
> All the petty worries and woes
> Are done.
> The soul stands alone, final product of
> My life.

Paul D. discovered *self-hatred* as his governing self-concept: "Here lies Paul D., dead at twenty-eight. He didn't love long enough because he spent his life worrying about the wrong things." His meaning is to be found in "worrying about the right things."

One young woman found her meaning in the struggle for *social justice.* "A civil libertarian and defender of social justice and staunch consumer advocate; active in affairs that supported my political ideology, including a concern for women's legal rights to self-determination and a passionate horticulturalist, especially my rose garden among other flowers. Belief in the widening and enriching horizons of knowledge through education. A fond lover of mate and family."

Roy discovered the meaning of life in the *idea of a home.* "Here lies a man that enjoyed his family and living."

Tanya wanted *peace:*

> She dreamed; she cried; she loved a few.
> Most of the time, she was at peace;
>   so be it now.

Let me conclude with Debra, who found in both the centeredness of individuality and the joy of intimacy the direction her life should take: "Love made her happy . . . happiest. Both giving and receiving. . . . But there was always the element of threat and fear that entered without question. Perhaps, if she had not spent so much time 'listening' to others, searching for the answers, she may have found more 'listening' to herself. In spite of all, she 'felt' and loved life!"

Alan Watts upon occasion used a very beautiful image. He talked of those of us who are always looking for health, searching for fulfillment, looking for beauty—in short, reaching *out to heaven.* Yet we often fail to realize that we exist already on a beautiful globe floating permanently in the heavens. We wish we were going to heaven, when in fact we are already there. Now ask yourself, why do not I take advantage of that fact? Why don't I achieve some realization of the full implications of that insight? I am already *in* the answer that I seek. When I confront the inevitability of death, I discover that my meaning is close at hand.

Let us consider Nellie B. again for a moment. When she became terminally ill she finally took the issue of finding meaning in life seriously. When she did not have a *real* problem—that is, death—she wasted her time by avoiding real issues. She played the game of *avoiding* meanings rather than searching for them. Only when she knew she was about to die did she become serious. And then she realized that her life had meaning, and she became joyous. She also realized that the fulfillment of her life was in *her* hands. It is as simple as that.

Now that we are in touch with the *experience* of confronting the anxiety of death, let us examine the reasons for discussing painful rather than pleasurable experiences as the beginning of a philosophy of life.

5

Sorrow or Joy:
Which Leads to Meaning?

FULFILLMENT THROUGH PAIN AND THROUGH JOY

I am often asked, "Why does existentialism seem to be a philosophy of despair? Can we not grasp joy directly? Must we first suffer through anxiety, guilt, and the fear of death?"

There are two basic approaches to enhancing the quality of life—the approach through *joy*, the optimistic approach, and the approach through *despair*, the pessimistic approach. Many writers represent the general view that joy can be grasped directly. The assumption is that if you only properly perceive, experience, think, or understand, then you will also realize that joy exists directly before you. In other words, joy is thought to be immediately available to anyone who knows how to take it. This position is popular, and it presents a marvelously hopeful and encouraging attitude. Occasionally all of us need to have the insight that joy is available to us all. Yet implicit in the power of positive thinking is the conviction that there exists a right kind of technique that will guarantee that we re-perceive the world in patterns of joy. We search for a gimmick, a trick, or a new way of seeing that makes the deathly silent black-and-white world of meaninglessness explode into the brilliant colors of meaning. Unfortunately, and in view of the complex tragedies and paradoxes of life, this purely positive approach is altogether too simplistic.

Let us look at three philosophies of joy: two Western approaches and an oriental one. The existential approach represented within this book must reject them all, because it uses the far more widespread phenomenon of anxiety instead of joy as its point of departure.

Some of the philosophies that defend a solely optimistic view of life are often artificial; they are epitomized first and most clearly, perhaps, by the Dale Carnegie and related schools of the power of positive thinking. You say to yourself that you are going to be positive, you are going to like everything, and you will succeed in remaking yourself to those sets of specifications which will insure success in all areas of your life. But such mechanical motivation does not spring from the depth of your inwardness; it resides only on the surface of your material extensions and possessions. Positive thinking, undoubtedly useful for limited purposes, is the "used-car salesman" approach to life. I have no intention of being unkind to the hard-sell salesman, because he is not necessarily a person of ill will. He does not adopt an artificial front, a veneer of joy and enthusiasm, because he is mean, hypocritical, or evil. He thinks he has no other choice. He believes his is a competitive, cutthroat world, and the only way he can exist in it is to "rise above it." The only way he can get through his often unhappy day is to tell himself convincingly that he is enthusiastic, that he loves his job, and that he is sold on his product. Thus he survives. There is a large turnover of such salesmen because their attitudes simply do not last—theirs is not a proper approach to a meaningful life.

A more authentic Western approach is the search for joy through the body. Joy is thought to be achieved by precipitating cathartic and sometimes traumatic emotional experiences. It can also be achieved by physical exercise, massage, and other forms of body manipulation, since the body is the seat of sensuality and thus of much pleasure and joy. These are modern versions of classical hedonistic and sybaritic philosophies. The burgeoning human potential movement is rich in examples of this approach. While I endorse these approaches, I believe that they are not complete in themselves—they do not respond to the tragic dimension of life, which must be addressed. If there is a difference between existentialism and humanistic psychology it is this: the latter focuses on joy whereas the former is particularly sensitive to the meaning-giving potential of the tragic dimension of life.

A third direct approach to the search for joy comes from what is essentially an oriental view. It is the contention that differences between good and evil are illusory, that the ego itself is an illusion and that the cosmos is one and all is right with the world. This is a religious or philosophical mysticism. Joy in this spirit involves the transcendence of material appearances, psychological states (such as emotions), and value differences (such as pleasure and pain). It is a philosophy of unqualified optimism; no pain or evil will be permitted to prove wrong its rosy metaphysics. I respect this approach to life. But it is not existential—although we will see later that existentialism can make room for it. I believe that in the end the depth of Eastern mysticism can be wedded to a philosophy of Western realism, but only after beginning with anxiety and despair—in short, with acknowledgement of death—as the real source of the search for meaning.

Existentialism, of course, recognizes that joy, peace, and freedom are in the nature of the person and that they accompany the discovery of meaning. But the existential way of life begins with a note of sadness resulting from a profound sense of appreciation for the seemingly endless suffering of mankind. The existential approach is less through joy or mysticism than it is through a thorough working-through of pain, suffering, meaninglessness, and anxiety. In a word: meaning comes from experiencing the *anxiety of death*. For Matthew Arnold, the ocean's waves

> . . . bring
> The eternal note of sadness in.
>
> Sophocles long ago
> Heard it on the Aegean, and it brought
> Into his mind the turbid ebb and flow
> Of human misery . . .

His philosophical starting point is existential, because the world itself

> Hath really neither joy, nor love, nor light,
> Nor certitude, nor peace, nor help for pain. . . . [1]

A solution to the sorrow-joy paradox is possible if we examine the concept of polarity as it applies to our search for meaning.

POLARITY

Let us be more specific and technical. Central to the existential view of human nature is the recognition of the fundamental "dialectic" of personal reality. We have discussed the fact that human existence consists of opposites, of polarities. Meaning is found not in the *choice between polarities* but in the experience of *wholeness* that derives from *integrating opposites* in the sense of complementarity. Life is a series of paradoxes. The sorrow-joy conflict is one. We can opt for their integration into a larger whole or choose one of the two extremes. All are authentic coping devices. Existentialism has had the tendency to *begin* with the option for sorrow. Everyone has to decide for himself which approach to fulfillment suits him best. Although searching for meaning

---

[1] "Dover Beach," from *The Works of Matthew Arnold,* ed. G. W. E. Russell (London: Macmillan, 1903-4), Vol. 2, p. 123.

or fulfillment through either pleasure or pain are, in an absolute sense, both "correct" paths to authenticity, the practical and therapeutic approach endorsed in this book starts with the pain of death.

The approach to human fulfillment through joy is the path of being *directly in touch with external reality* and identifying with it. Conversely, the approach to human fulfillment through pain is the path of *distance from and reflection on external reality*. The first path—that of pleasure or hedonism—belongs to intemperate and exuberant youth. It can be foolhardy, arrogant, self-centered, and full of risks, but it is also joyous and sublime. The second path—of distance and stoicism—is that of reason and maturity. It is wise and it endures. It is humble and modest; it is compassionate and just. These paths represent the polarity of lifestyles.

We in our conscious selves can favor one of two attitudes toward existence, thereby generating a lifestyle. One attitude is to be involved, committed, and identified—leading to a sense of being in touch with what is real and to a sense of joy. The other is to be detached or removed from direct and practical touch with the world that is external to the conscious inwardness that I am. This is a lifestyle of observation and reflection rather than of commitment. Both lifestyles, of commitment and detachment, are legitimate human attitudes, as would also be true of a life of integration. Through both we can work for the fulfillment of our potential; and when we talk of death, we also talk of the answer that death gives us to our passionate search for joy. But likewise, when we talk of joy, we know it must come to an end. Therefore, both approaches to meaning, the positive and negative, are interrelated and intertwined. Very few people are at the extreme ends of this continuum—most of us are varying mixtures of these attitudes, with perhaps a dominance of one or the other.

A COMPARISON OF APPROACHES

Let me illustrate the difference between these two poles—the "hedonistic" approach to life (the search for meaning and fulfillment through "being in touch" and through joy, which is the "positive" approach—the practical, engaged, involved and committed attitude) and the "ascetic" approach (the search for fulfillment through detachment, observation, reflection, and nonparticipation). The purely ascetic lifestyle is aesthetic, artistic, and contemplative. That important distinction can be clarified by talking about two entirely different ways color, such as red, can be perceived.

The color red may mean something practical. It may mean something "committed"—having to do with practical activity—as with a red traffic light. You see a red light in your car's rear-view mirror, and you stop. In this case, a red light means danger, caution, stop: and you act upon that meaning. There is nothing artistic about that red light—it is part of your daily activities.

But there is another way to perceive the color red. That is the aesthetic or the detached way. We may have several reds around us: the red of a book, the red of a rose, the red of a house and of the sun. We can look at these various reds as an artist would, aesthetically, and ask ourselves what kind of red is it? What *meaning* does it have? What can it symbolize? What are its emotional associations? In this way we have moved from the practical attitude, where red means danger, to the artistic attitude, where red is thought of as raw material for artistic creation.

In existential philosphy we call the first type of perception the *engaged* or the *natural attitude*. It represents the hedonistic or the committed lifestyle. It is the practical attitude; in it we are *conscious of* our world but not *self*-conscious. The second kind of seeing we call *reflection* or *stepping back*. That attitude corresponds to the ascetic or distanced lifestyle.

In managing death we must emphasize the *self*-conscious aspect of consciousness. This self-conscious focus shows us the nature of our consciousness, and is the ascetic attitude. The arts represent a similar way of looking and lifestyle. In the aesthetic attitude the object ceases to be practical and is observed self-consciously. Through asceticism and art, then, we eventually discover consciousness for what it really is.

A second illustration that can help us understand these two different attitudes or acts of consciousness—the committed (positive, joy) and the detached (negative, pain)—is to examine the experience of sound. Imagine the total sound of a train approaching a railroad crossing: the bells, the rattle of the wheels, the squeal of brakes, and the powerful sounds of the passing train itself. Picture the locomotive racing with its concatenation of clanking cars. If you should be driving a car approaching the intersection, and especially if your brakes are poor, the sounds of the oncoming train are danger signals. You make sure you stop before you reach the tracks. Under these circumstances the sound is experienced in a *practical* context and you are *in touch* with the world. Your consciousness is lost in the world, attached to it; you are committed to it. This approach to life in general I called, for lack of a better word, the "hedonistic" approach—the approach in which you are in touch with and identified with reality. This perspective represents confidence in the body and faith in the goodness and order of the world.

There is another way of experiencing the sound, a way that is not practical, but *detached*—this attitude is certainly not to be recommended when you are approaching a railroad crossing. This spectatorial or aesthetic type of perception makes you listen to and reflect on the *quality* of the sound. You recognize that the sound is rich in nuances and detail; you perceive that there are parts that are harsh, metallic, grinding, threatening, and non-human. But you also hear that there are parts that are mellow, soft, warm, and attractive. Furthermore, there are aspects of the total sound that constantly change—making a whole mosaic of sound. That is how a musician, perhaps a composer, might hear the sound of the train passing through a railroad crossing. He observes rather than participates. His awareness is self-conscious and aesthetic rather than world-conscious and practical.

The latter approach to life's meaning and fulfillment is negative and existential, whereas the first one we described is positive and manipulative. Both have their uses. The existential is both less common and more powerful. Existentialism as a philosophy of anxiety and death has a cynical foundation. Its point of departure is frustration, betrayal, and disappointment. Strength, in existentialism, derives from the detached inward and free consciousness of man, a fortress that can withstand all storms but that makes it possible for us to be safe on the day the sun comes out.

An authentic person finds it necessary to seek fulfillment both ways and to recognize that *both commitment and detachment are genuine human possibilities.* That is the position emphasized in this book.

The distinction between the attached and the detached modes of consciousness is fundamental to our understanding of all aspects of human existence. This lengthy preliminary, as any responsible philosophical analysis must do, serves therefore to place the discussion of pain and anxiety in its proper perspective.

DESPAIR

How can philosophy be used for the management of life from the negative point of view—from the point of view of pain? In our search for meaning, our point of departure is the ever-present reality of anxiety. I choose this approach not only because it is existential but also because I want to deal with all negative aspects of life: despair, unhappiness, misery, depression, death, guilt, loneliness, and meaningless-ness—and deal with them philosophically. Compassion and consolation are traditional in the history of philosophy. Pain—especially the anxiety of death—is a condition of human life, an experience of being human which enables us to sustain, extend, and deepen our humanity through detachment. That is the clue to the whole existential approach to death.

Let us now proceed to a more detailed analysis of the structure of the anxiety of death.

6

The Structure of Anxiety:
Polarity
and Consciousness

PILLS VERSUS PHILOSOPHY

Existential philosophy has been fertilized by anxiety. It was developed in response to the pervasive existence of anxiety and can help us come to terms with that anxiety. And anxiety, as we have been saying in the first five chapters, can be explored best through a direct confrontation with the experience of death.

Death, although real to us, is never experienced directly and we thus have only indirect knowledge of it. Nevertheless, our anxiety about death can reveal to us especially the nature and reality of our consciousness. In Part Three we will examine the problem of understanding and experiencing consciousness itself, which is a most important task because it contains the promise and the hope of an answer to death.

Defining death's meaning is difficult, in part because dying is an aspect of life itself. The statement "all living is a form of dying" is an accurate definition of both dying and living. In ordinary language and in the world of common sense we *expel* the act of dying from our actual living in the here and now. Our language and belief systems brainwash us into the conviction that death is a foreign land, a distant planet inaccessible to the immediate and present reality of the here and now—which is all that we rather naively identify with life. We do not realize that in truth living and dying are complementary, yin–yang aspects of one continuous and integrated field of consciousness.

It is this attempt to escape from the life–death polarity of our actual present experience of existing that is implicit in the connotations of the word "dying." The same is true of words like "suicide" and "insanity." These are words that are meant to apply to *other* people or to later (out-of-reach) conditions of myself. For example, dying is something that will happen to me *later*. It is a reality that I force away from the present. That is how language, common sense, and the life-world try to protect me from the anxiety of living, which is really the anxiety about death. The truth is, I am dying right now. I am dying right now in the same sense that I shall always be dying. I am at this precise moment moving to my death in essentially the same way that I always have and always will be. But to admit that I am directed toward death is also to experience the fullness of living. There is anxiety in this polarity. But instead of acknowledging and seeking to understand this anxiety we avoid it by taking pills and by inventing mechanical ways to find meaning. And we compulsively postpone the realization that we are dying. Unfortunately, what this also does is to postpone our living.

We want to find an answer to death from this perspective of polarity. We are in effect looking for a cure to anxiety, anguish, and despair. Anxiety may well be the greatest mental health problem of our day. And because we adopt in our culture what I call a "ghost-in-a-machine" theory of human beings—that is, a mechanistic, technological, and materialistic approach to ourselves and others—rather than a field-of-consciousness theory, we believe that we can deal with anxiety, pain, suffering, and despair as we would handle malfunctions in machines. It is this mechanistic approach to solutions that is part of the problem in the first place. We seek to cure death instead of searching out the knowledge that death is a part of life.

In a machine, if there is a loose screw, you can fix the problem by replacing or tightening the screw. Similarly, we use pills for emotional problems, in which case those problems are handled *for* us and not *by* us. You don't think about managing the anxiety about death—someone else, physician or pharmacist, is always there to take the responsibility of dealing with it for you. Thus you perceive anxiety as a problem external to you rather than an integral part of your consciousness itself. As a result, you seek external object manipulations to solve your problems, rather than assuming personal responsibility for integrating the experience of dying into living. The person who sees death as external is fragmented. He who perceives death as part of life is integrated and whole.

If we cannot sleep we take a pill. If we feel anxious, we take a pill. If we have a headache, we take a pill. The pain is forced away, we become dulled and tranquilized. But in a lobotomy, this tranquility is purchased at the price of diminished humanity. Once we take the life-death polarity out of the experience of existing, we substitute vegetation for personhood, drifting for agency, and passivity for direction.

The attitude that either a mechanical, material thing or another person can do the living for you, can take over your responsibility for being alive, is a pervasive one in our culture. It is the direct result of the belief that a human being is a thing rather than an inwardness, an object rather than a subject—a ghost in a machine.

A friend of mine owns a small drugstore. In the morning he opens a bottle containing 500 Valium tablets (tranquilizers) and by noon it is empty. On Fridays, his customers call him up and come in, afraid that they will not have enough medicine for the weekend. It is a sad situation.

So we see that there are two ways to manage anxiety: through pills or through philosophy. To attempt to cope with our problems by using pills is the manipulative, mechanical, technological approach to living. It is a degradation, a denial and betrayal of being human. But there is a way of living or approaching human problems that seeks self-knowledge, self-disclosure and, in the words of Nietzsche, "becoming what one is." And negative experiences, such as anxiety about death, play a crucial role in such a philosophy.

Let us now focus more sharply on a description and definition of anxiety.

SEPARATION ANXIETY AND CONSCIOUSNESS

Death reveals the existence and structure of my consciousness. Only through the reminder of death do I understand that *I am more than a body, more than a personality, more than a name*—I am also a consciousness, one that is aware *of* my body, *of* my personality and *of* my name, but is not to be confused with them. Consciousness is not a thought but an experience, not a concept but an accessible region of being, and that experience can only be apprehended through direct confrontation of the death of myself. There are many ways to disclose the constant, solitary, and silent center that we are. We will explore several approaches.

The important concept of *separation anxiety* is meaningful—a facilitating idea—in the disclosure of consciousness and to illustrate the fact that this disclosure is inevitably an anxiety-producing phenomenon. Separation anxiety—the fear of being dislodged, abandoned—is a pervasive fear. Think of a little child who sees his mother take her car out of the garage to park it at the curb, and immediately cries, "Mommy, where are you going?" That is separation anxiety. Death symbolizes separation from life. Thus the fear of death is the fear of separation from life.

In World War II, young children were separated from their parents and sent to the country for their own safety; however, they suffered far more emotional damage than the children who were permitted to stay with their parents. For them, separation did more harm than fear of injury from the bombing. A *practical* concern for their physical well-being overshadowed the more important concern for their emotional health.

Some people, who are inordinately threatened by any suggestion of separation, may compensate for this fear by remaining permanently separate or alienated so as never to undergo the process of separation. Separation anxiety is not unrelated to castration anxiety, which is of course also a form of separation.

The fear of being separated from life through death is really the asymptotic or limit experience of pure consciousness. The following illustration should help to put you in touch with the *experience* rather than only the concept of pure consciousness.

Think of yourself as being in a state of total and complete attachment to something. Think of yourself as being a small child, perhaps, wholly attached to your mother. Most adults have lost the sense of how all-encompassing that attachment really is. We forget that a child knows nothing of this world—he is ignorant of even the most basic forms in which adults perceive the world. And for him his mother is all there is—from her, from her behavior, her reaction to him, he learns what the world is like and he never forgets it.

You are now that little child; you are not *self-*conscious; you are only *object-*conscious. You are toothless, wordless, only able to suck, defecate, and cry; your mother is your world, and your whole being is a reaching out, an emerging, or a transcendence from "here" out to "Mother." You do not know that you are a child. You do not even know that you exist. All you know is that the objects of your consciousness, the objects of your perception, exist. You are totally identified with your objects. There is no residue of inwardness, independence, or inner strength. You are totally absorbed in the objects before you: mother, mother, and more mother.[1]

Putting yourself in this position of complete involvement is difficult, because as adults we tend to be reserved, controlled, and rather ra-

---

[1] Think of how children behave at the movies. The minute the movie starts, the pop-corn-eating stops and the children are all absorbed in looking at the film, totally impervious to the fact that they exist also as separate entities themselves. If the protagonist is

tional, and we rarely abandon ourselves totally—except perhaps when we are hopelessly inebriated. Imagine yourself being such a child, totally identified with what you see and feel, and having *no inner resources.* Mother feeds, mother cuddles, mother changes; she sings, tucks in, diapers, and so on. Mother is the world. The "I" does not yet exist—if it is anything at all, it is a cosmic "Mother." If now the *mother is removed,* then suddenly *your world has disappeared.* And that is like death. But note that in this case you also *know (sense)* that the world has disappeared, whereas in "real" death, we assume, the *knowledge* and the *sensation* of death also disappear. The child suffering from separation thus experiences a *living death.* What is that?

What remains is what in phenomenology we call a "pure look." You suddenly discover something that was always true but of which you were not conscious—that is, it is something you have been looking at all the time. In other words, you were not *self*-conscious. You are now left with your look. You are now forced by the circumstances of the separation or severance to become aware of your "looking." And that looking in search of an object, that objectless consciousness, is your *pure awareness* ("transcendental consciousness," in the jargon of phenomenology). Everything that the look had seen has ceased to be, disappeared. That kind of experience is accompanied by tremendous anxiety. You are grabbing onto something and then it is gone. You are left with a pure look, with your pure consciousness. That is pure anxiety and that is pure consciousness. The two seem to be inextricably intertwined. This will be dealt with in more detail in Part Three.

I want you to develop a sense of the fierce and desperate attachment to the world exemplified by the child's attachment to his mother. If you were able to imagine yourself as a dependent infant, intensely attached to your mother, you may have been able to experience the sheer panic of "letting go." "Letting go" produces extreme anxiety as well as a knowledge about the pure consciousness that you are. This exercise may have given you an insight into this anxiety connected with letting go—which in reality is the threat of non-being or nothingness.

To one who is totally engrossed with the objects of this world, the discovery that he is also a consciousness is an experience of supreme anxiety. And thus death is the ultimate symbol of anxiety—the separation from life itself—and it reveals to us the meaning of consciousness.

"good" they love him, and when the villain enters they boo at him. They are totally involved in the movie; if someone on the screen should ask the audience a question, they will loudly respond en masse.

The fundamental cognitive device in existential thought is anxiety. Thus, anxiety is not principally an emotion; it is not an unconscious conflict, nor is it necessarily psychopathology. Anxiety is not unconscious material threatening the defenses of the ego. It is the *immediate disclosure of consciousness in itself.* It is a cognitive, revealing, informing phenomenon. Nothing helps us achieve the insight into the structure of consciousness better than death and the anxiety about death.

Now that we have explored one aspect of the structure of the anxiety of death, we can move on to the more specific topic of pain.

7

Death as Answer
to Pain and Evil

A TEST FOR PAIN

The question of a possible answer to death involves us in a general discussion of pain. I prefer to use the general term "negative experiences" but the word "pain" is generally better understood. Negative and painful experiences, of which death is our most dramatic illustration, must be taken seriously. We must remember that there is a philosophic meaning to pain. We do not understand it if we restrict ourselves to medical or psychological models, however. Pain is not always associated with a disease; it is an aspect of human existence. In fact, pain may well be the essential ingredient in our human nature.

Pain is philosophically important because it is a teacher, a light, an opening door—in short, it can give us *understanding*. In one of Alan Watts' metaphors, he says that we usually see the world through a stained-glass window. Because the craftsmanship is artistic we have a beautiful vision—but we see the world distorted, nevertheless. To have an unobstructed view of the world, with the window wide open, is true philosophical enlightenment. It is through death and pain that those stained-glass windows are opened to the truth about you and your humanity. You do not know what it means to be human, you do not know the essence of your humanity, unless you have opened the window to your nature. And this window can be opened only through the knowledge provided by suffering: pain, death and all the negative experiences of life. That is an ancient truth. Suffering leads to insight, to knowledge about what it really means for us to *be*.

We discussed in the previous chapter that one way of achieving knowledge about human existence is through experiencing joy. But we emphasized that another way, the existential way, of achieving knowledge about human beings is through suffering or, more accurately, through the exploration of negative experiences. Thus, suffering is a philosophical methodology, a scientific approach, the conclusion of which is the knowledge of the human condition. Death puts you in direct touch with what is real.

I have developed a "pain test" that measures the amount of philosophically relevant pain in a person's life.[1] These pains are anxiety, guilt, physical pain, tragedy, depression, meaninglessness, loneliness, and frustration. A profile is developed by analyzing self-ratings from a list of 285 alphabetically-listed adjectives such as accepted, accomplished, achieving, aching, etc. The test consists of eight subtests, because I believe there are eight different kinds of pain and that each one has its own unique way of leading us to the truth about personality. If, for example, you are a person who experiences a below-average amount of pain, as measured by this test, then your approach to meaning is probably through joy. On the other hand, if your amount of pain is far above average then your approach to meaning is probably through pain. We have in this existential approach an important therapeutic insight and strategy.

Furthermore, because the test discriminates among eight types of philosophically relevant pains, it can tell the individual which of the eight types of pain he might find most useful as a point of departure for creating meaning in his life. Is it loneliness, depression, meaninglessness, anxiety or despair, guilt, physical pain, death, or is it tragedy or conflict? I believe, for example, that loneliness is the experience of the uniqueness of being you. And anxiety can show you something about the reality and then the eternity of your consciousness, as we have discussed. A scrutiny of guilt can open up insights about your freedom. Whatever pain is most pronounced in your life is the area in which you can start an examination on how you personally can find meaning in life, because the maximum pain discloses that personality structure which in you needs most attention.

Many of my students have taken the pain test. The test contains pain words, such as *aggravated, hostile, angry, suffering, arthritic,* and pleasure words, such as *sexy, passionate, happy, joyous,* and so on. One tangential discovery I made is that a person who thinks of himself as, for example, arthritic also thinks of himself as experiencing *less pain* than a person who does not perceive himself as arthritic. Generalizing, we can hypothesize that—in terms of self-image—a person who is in this

[1] See *Managing Anxiety,* Part 2 (Englewood Cliffs, N.J.: Prentice-Hall, Inc., 1974).

type of pain may be able to make more sense out of his life than a person who does not have opened for him this window to his human nature. I also discovered that a person who defines himself as "sexy" and "passionate" tends to experience greater pain than one who does not perceive himself as such. The hypothesis suggests itself that sex may be for some an escape from pain rather than an expression of joy. The emphasis on sexuality and the mutual orgasm in the sex act as *sine qua non* for a meaningful life has been unduly exaggerated by our society. Death is more important than sex in understanding the truth about human existence, and anxiety is more important than passion for finding meaning in life.

TRANSLATING PAIN INTO MEANING

Frankl

Negative experiences—such as the anxiety about death—are constructive because they can *lead to meaning*. How does this transition take place? We learn not to fight or silence the pain but get into it. We allow the pain (and I do not mean physical pain but pain in general) to be; we allow it to speak to us. When we allow that to happen our pain reveals to us what condition we must fight, what evil we must oppose, so as to conquer it. It is in this struggle that we find our meaning in life. Thus pain leads first to understanding and then to meaning. Viktor Frankl's logotherapy also is based on the idea that in our greatest pain we can also find our deepest meaning; it is, in fact, in the attempt to understand our pain and oppose and conquer it that we will find our answer to the question of the meaning of life. The meaning of life is the conquest of negation, the conquest of suffering, the management of finitude—the answer to death. Thus, the conquest of death, victory over death, the struggle against death—these become central issues in man's quest for fulfillment and joy. In this way the emphasis on the negative can indeed lead to positive results.

The Daughter

One of Frankl's followers gives the following illustration of the meaning-giving power of death. The story and its analysis appeared in the *Journal of Existentialism* many years ago, and I recall only the general outline. It described a man whose young daughter had been sexually assaulted and murdered. The real horror of that kind of situation, its unspeakable tragedy, was of course something that only this father could fully know. To try to make some sense out of the wreckage of his life, and to keep from committing suicide, this man sought the help of a therapist.

The therapist knew that this father was suffering from a condition for which there is no answer. In his case, anything that pretended to be an answer would in reality have represented the height of insensitivity. Any message from the therapist on the order of "You can get over it—you can adjust to it—you'll forget about it" would have compounded the felony by making the father a co-conspirator, an accessory to the crime. It would have been wrong to have urged him to adjust, to accept the unacceptable. Anything like a "solution" to the problem "What shall I do with my agony?" is in truth worse than nothing.

After the father had spent some time talking about and ventilating his pain, it gradually became less, and slowly his despair abated. The therapist had not however touched on the real issue. Three years later, the father went back to the grave of his daughter with an offering of flowers. He reflected on how he had spent his last three years: gradually trying to adjust to the reality of her death. And he began to feel very guilty. He believed that this "adjustment" meant that she had died in vain. There, kneeling at the grave, she was still real to him, and he felt he had betrayed her by accepting her tragic end. With his life he had said, in effect, "It's all right, such terrible things happen, and let's not worry about them too much."

At that moment something exploded within him that was quite beyond the therapy he had received; he resolved that the only proper response to her death was one of outrage. That was the existential situation. He decided to contribute his utmost to the goal that such things should never happen again. And the selfless, aggressive pursuit of that angry ideal gave the father a meaning he had never had before. Through his subsequent fight against evil and crime, his life acquired purpose and significance. In his decision to use his outrage and pain as stepping stones to purposeful strength, he moved out of pain and toward meaning.

Someone who tells you that you can adjust to the agony of a horrible, unsolvable, and painful experience has an inexcusably dehumanizing attitude. The authentic human response to having your child killed ought to be one of uncompromising outrage—certainly not one of attempted adjustment to an awful occurrence. The proper response to

evil is outrage and not adjustment; it is fight and not acceptance. This
tells us that in a person's very rebellion against pain is the seed of his
understanding of the meaning of life.

What is the purpose of life? Is it joy or happiness? Not really. It is
discovering the meaning of one's own existence. By the example of
the agonized father it is made clearer that in the very struggle to manage negative experiences we can in fact begin to find this meaning.

The Son

There is another, similar illustration of this idea. Some years ago
there was a man in California whose son, just graduated from college,
was killed by a drunk driver. His son was dead due to the irresponsi-
bility of another person. This man traveled across the state of California pulling his son's demolished car on a trailer, agitating for stiff anti-
drunk driving legislation. And partially thanks to his single-minded,
patient, relentless efforts, the state of California now has some of the
nation's stiffest laws against drunk driving. Nothing could ever compensate for his son's death, but this father made certain that his son
did not die in vain. And in pursuit of that goal he found the meaning
of his life.

PAIN AS SELF-WILLED

Responsibility

In addition to understanding and meaning, pain leads to *responsibility*. Each of us can take responsibility for his pain. Pain, specifically negation and death, is an integral part of human existence. Human nature could never be what it is without the presence of pain and death.
The creation of a human being in his full glory requires the concurrent creation of pain and death. This point is as difficult to make with
clarity as it is important that it be understood. I do not want to adopt
a medieval religious viewpoint, one that says evil is good, but I want
nevertheless to discuss this strategy by reference to what may be an
outdated medieval viewpoint. In fact, I need to refer to two philosophic positions, one medieval and the other from the Age of Reason.
Dante can illustrate the medieval position and Leibniz the rationalist
view.

Leibniz

Leibniz was well known as an apologist for the status quo, very
much in the tradition of Alexander Pope, who wrote, in his *Essay on
Man,* "Whatever is, is right." This acquiescing theme, one of theodicy,
is also found in Milton's "Paradise Lost," and in the Bible's *Book of
Job.* All these are efforts to justify the existence of evil in a world that
has presumably been created by an all-powerful and an all-good God.
Theologians and all religious people have had the problem of recon-
ciling the existence of such a God with the inescapable reality of evil
in the world. This problem must be dealt with in any attempts, philosophical or theological, to understand death. Leibniz argued that this
is the best of all possible worlds. He was ridiculed for this idea by
Voltaire in *Candide.* Leibniz maintained, in effect, that we are responsible for making sense of the evil in the world. We must reperceive evil
as having been placed before us to enable us to achieve a worthwhile
end. It is our task to find the key that will turn even the most unconscionable evil into an agency for good.

The ancient theological problem of evil is really the contemporary
existential problem of pain and death. Medieval theology can give us a
clue to a contemporary existential understanding of evil. For some medieval theologians evil is a necessary and a good part of the Divine
Plan. This view is not as callous as it may seem. It is part of a profound strategy for dealing with evil. Unless you can accept that in
some mysterious way evil is part of the whole plan of life, you cannot
survive with any sense of dignity and meaning in this world.

Dante

This strategy of integrating negative experiences such as death into
a whole life says that evil is in some perhaps inexplicable way a com-
ponent of value. Since death is our most obvious and dramatic evil, we
must take personal responsibility for death. The answer to death is
that you want it that way, even to the extent that you are personally
responsible for death; and the reason for your responsibility is that
evil is an essential part of life's true meaning. That approach to the
management of negative experiences I call the medieval approach. Its
symbolism contains more truth in it than at first appears.

These ideas are expressed with forceful clarity in the inscription that
Dante saw when Virgil took him to Hell. Most people remember the

famous lines from the gates of the Inferno, "Abandon every hope, you who enter here." But the lines that precede this are really astounding:

> Justice moved my exalted creator;
> The divine power made me,
> The supreme wisdom, and the primal love,
> Before me all created things were eternal,
> And eternal I will last.
> Abandon every hope, you who enter here.

Dante represented the world view of medieval Europe. And he argued that even this awful place, this hell, where all the imaginable and unimaginable tortures of mankind are collected, is the result of God's great wisdom and great love!

You are free to reject that view as arrant nonsense, as the perverse rationalization of a sick mind. But it is also possible to see a deeper truth in this symbolism of evil—that Dante has developed a metaphor about man's best strategy for dealing with evil.

In other words, evil is so horrendous, so utterly unacceptable that we absolutely must find some way to explain it so that we can hope for moral survival and meaning in life. And one way to make sense of evil is to say it is part of the larger design of being and that being in its totality is good. The position I represent can be reduced to the following basic elements.

Responsibility for Evil

If I were God, a being of infinite compassion and power, and had the power to create a universe, I would create a world in which the existence of evil—and thus by implication the overcoming of evil—would be the fundamental program of nature. Finally, I, as God, would recognize this completed world to be a good world. The world is blessed with life, since life is but the eternal *process* through which the unending struggle to overcome evil is guaranteed. That seemingly perverse and ancient message permits us to come to terms with that with which we cannot really come to terms—namely, irrevocable evil, including death.

I often start my classes by asking students to write down a problem which, like William James' "genuine option," is *unbearable* in its agony but has *no* solutions. In such a problem is the kind of evil that Dante's *Inferno* describes. That is the kind of situation for which we need philosophy. It is evil without redemption, yet we as authentic persons are determined to come to terms with it. We have made the decision to survive as human beings, which implies that *we have chosen the impossible: to come to terms with evil.* Herein lies the nobility of the human spirit. We are *determined* to find meaning in evil; thus we *decide* that evil has a place in the nature of things. We do not accept evil—we do not further it, condone it, nor are we indifferent to it. Instead, we choose that the existence of evil make sense, and we choose not to become evil either by becoming insane or by allying ourselves with that evil. We choose to insist that we will make a humane, compassionate use of evil. The decision to make sense of evil is to consider it part of a larger good. Difficult as that decision may be, it is a necessary strategy if we are to make sense of evil, suffering, pain, death.

Let us now return to the one specific evil which concerns us in this book—namely, death. We can carry out resolutely the philosophical decision to demand that the evil of death have meaning by considering typical ways in which people accept and take responsibility for death.

PSYCHOLOGICAL ATTITUDES TOWARD DEATH

One way human beings have of making death meaningful is to develop *symbols* for death. Kastenbaum's excellent research[2] shows that certain symbolic ideas recur. One is the notion that death is *macabre.* Another pictures death as the *gentle comforter.* The third typical symbol is death as a *gay deceiver.* Finally, death is seen as mechanical, cold, insensitive, and impersonal: *an automaton.*

Kastenbaum points out that the meaning of death depends on the *social setting.* We are suggestible; therefore the mood—that is to say, the affective quality of death—is *learned.* The anxiety about death is in part a social phenomenon.

Growing up in our culture teaches us that death is *real, is, exists.* It also teaches us *how to experience* death. Finally, it tells us how much *adjustment* to death is proper and how much is not. And we are taught *how to carry out* that adjustment.

Do we experience death as something natural? Unnatural? Fortunate or unfortunate? Can we accept it? Is it fair or unfair? Our attitude toward death is not automatically one of anguish or anxiety. The anxiety response may, at least in part, be learned. Analyzing our own response can teach us how to take personal responsibility for managing the evil of death.

We can also respond to death by *avoiding* responsibility.

[2]Robert Kastenbaum, *The Psychology of Death* (New York: Springer, 1972).

Avoidance Responses to Death

The responses to death discussed in my book *The Vitality of Death*[3] are philosophically derived; their logic is intuitive. Kastenbaum is a psychologist; he therefore does not investigate through philosophical means, but by means of questionnaires and related empirical, statistical studies.

Kastenbaum finds that the most common response to impending death is *depression*. It means to give up, not to fight death. This view is the opposite of the existential approach. In existentialism, as we have discussed, confronting death enables us to find meaning and fulfillment. Most people, however, do *not* respond to death authentically by saying, in effect, "I have to complete the unfinished business of my life—I must make sense of my life now." On the contrary, the common response is inauthentic: "What is the use of living? Why wait a year? Why not kill myself today?"

A second response to death Kastenbaum calls *displacement*. We do not accept death; we translate it into something else. We do not experience it *with us*, but elsewhere. We project death, pushing it aside so we will not see it. In the words of Martin Heidegger, "Death is just beyond the horizon."

A third response to death is *fear*, which can become despair and panic. This is a reaction of direct avoidance.

But in existentialism, death is a compressed statement of an anxiety that is even beyond the fear of death. We can therefore expand Kastenbaum's psychological observation into a deeper and universal philosophical disclosure. Fear, as response to death, translates into anxiety and thereby can be used to help us discover the foundation of human existence. The foundation phenomenon of human existence is anxiety precisely because anxiety is rooted in the discovery and experience of foundationlessness, groundlessness, an eternal falling in infinite empty space. It is a phenomenon of not being anything at all. The dramatic and behavioral "acting out" of this phenomenon is the fear of death. Death is but a symbol for this pervasive and underlying anxiety, an anxiety which reveals the essence of human existence. Kierkegaard describes the agony of anxiety and its relation to death in these powerful words from *The Sickness Unto Death,*

> The sickness unto death . . . means a sickness the end and outcome of which is
> death. . . . Yet in another and still more definite sense despair is the sickness unto

[3]Westport, Conn.: Greenwood, 1971.

death. . . . The torment of despair is precisely this, not to be able to die. So it has much in common with the situation of the moribund when he lies and struggles with death, and cannot die. So to be sick unto death is, not to be able to die—yet not as though there were hope of life; no, the hopelessness in this case is that even the last hope, death, is not available. When death is the greatest danger, one hopes for life; but when one becomes acquainted with an even more dreadful danger, one hopes for death. So when the danger is so great that death has become one's hope, despair is the disconsolateness of not being able to die.[4]

I use the word "death" to designate that sickness.

Death in itself is not necessarily tragic; but what *is* tragic is the *need* for a ground and the discovery of its *nonexistence.* Death therefore is in fact the *social symbol* for that fearsome, desperate, and lonely groundlessness. If there is a ground, that ground is consciousness; it is the source of all growth, creativity, and strength. It is also, in the words of Tillich, that which has the capacity to incorporate non-being into itself.

Other common responses to death mentioned by Kastenbaum are more authentic. And these can be interpreted existentially.

Authentic Responses

Another attitude toward death—one that is a healthier and more authentic response—is *sorrowing,* which differs from fear in that it is a more religious, aesthetic, and compassionate experience than is the panic associated with fear. To recognize the tragedy of life is a sobering aesthetic perception, but this is not terror. A person in a state of panic is dehumanized; a person confronting tragedy can be a noble hero.

A more demanding response to death is to *overcome* it. All three—fear, sorrowing, and overcoming—reveal the essential structures of human existence, but overcoming is perhaps the most difficult to achieve. To overcome death is to conquer it; and that goal is one of the great philosophical functions of religion. Some people may be able to overcome the anxiety of dying through philosophy, through just plain inner strength, through the inspiring example of a significant person or through dedication to causes, ideals, or other persons that will live beyond them.

Finally, one can respond to death with a desire to *participate:* death is an adventure, it is one of the interesting events of life. In this response the person says, "I want to be a part of my own death. I want to arrange my funeral. I want to be with my family when I die. I want to discuss my death with people important to me. As I participate in

[4] Translated by Walter Lowrie (New York: Doubleday, 1955).

birth, weddings, and other vital ceremonies of living, so I also wish to participate in my own death."

In our culture participation in death is perhaps the most foreign of all responses. Our culture relegates participation in a person's death to experts, such as physicians and morticians; people are encouraged to *avoid* thinking about or dealing with their own death. Participation, however, is characteristic of many primitive cultures, where death is often early and where people are personally involved in not only the death of others, but in their own as well.

This ends our discussion of strategies for fulfillment in life which start not with joy, but with pain. In order to accentuate this analysis by relating it to experience, let us move on to another exercise.

8

Death Exercises

Discussions of death can be intensified and made experiential in a variety of ways. Exercises on death can stimulate you to take the thought of *your* death seriously, and no longer think of your death as if it were that of someone else. When someone else dies, something in you dies as well: the part of you that has died is also a form of *your* death. However, you will not find any meaningful discussion of death that does not make the distinction between the death of another and the death of yourself, and make it sharply. These two experiences are different in kind, not just in intensity. In other words, these (and other) exercises evoke the experience of your own death and not that of another. Although most thoughts we have about death really concern the death of another, and thus represent escapist thinking, the following exercises will deal with your death alone.

BOBBY

Read the following story.

FAREWELL, BOBBY—WE LOVE YOU

It rained the day a little boy went to his grave.
But the sprinkles that fell were no match for the tears shed at his funeral Tuesday.
The strong and the brave wept openly for 6-year-old Bobby Chew, a frail waif who died without a family last Saturday of a muscle-crippling disease.
"He was our kid, we all knew and loved him," said one of a hundred noon-

time mourners who gathered in the dimly lighted cathedral-beamed chapel to say goodbye to the little guy.

Bobby, the blue-eyed, blond boy with the smiling face and undaunted spirit, would have loved the attention.

A native of San Jose, he was born with Hoffman's disease, which sapped his strength most of his life.

But he had another, probably even worse, handicap.

Never Knew Real Parents

Bobby never really knew his mother and father. If he remembered them at all it was faintly, because they abandoned him when he was two and one-half years old.

A ward of the court, he had no family, no relatives, no home. Nobody claimed him as their own until he found a "home" at Valley Medical Center where his illness required constant attention.

Doctors and nurses, long grown callous by the daily drama of life and death in a large hospital, fell desperately in love with the boy without a family.

"Everyone got involved," said Mrs. Christine Brock of the Junior Volunteers. "He was known throughout the hospital.

"He was just a darling boy, a real lovable little guy . . . "

She wanted to say more but a lump clutched her throat and the words didn't come.

Many Tender Memories

For her and the others who sat in tear-stained silence during his funeral there were too many tender memories.

Memories of wheelchair-bound Bobby greeting all ward visitors with a big hello. ("He signed up everybody in his guest register.")

Memories of Bobby poring over third grade math and science books. ("He was a very bright little boy.")

Memories of a younger Bobby pleading with nurses to read him a story. ("He always picked the longest story.")

And memories of his happy face when he was tucked into bed each night. ("The face of an angel.")

Bobby probably only wished for three things in life—a trip to Disneyland, a typewriter and, deep down inside, a chance to meet his real parents.

His first two wishes came true at Christmas, 1968, when the hospital's staff and work force chipped in, sent him to Disneyland and welcomed him back with a typewriter.

Bobby's third wish never came true, not exactly.

When other children used to teasingly ask about his parents, Bobby, chin-up always, would bravely reply:

"They live too far away to come and see me."

Something strange happened at his funeral.

In the front pew of the nearly filled chapel two strangers sat. If they cried no one could tell because no one who walked by bothered to look their way.

The strangers were Bobby's parents, the priest said. They'd read about Bobby's death in the newspaper, someone else said. This is a sad day for us, a member of his hospital family said.

The prodigal parents didn't say a word.

But Bobby's cherubic face in death held a slight smile—the sort of smile that lets you know everything is getting better.

It rained the day they buried Bobby; for his family it may never stop.[1]

After you have finished reading, complete the following seven sentences. Many of my students have found deep emotions and helpful insights about life's values through this exercise.

1. Reading about this tragedy made me feel that _____ .
2. What hurts me most about this tragedy is _____ .
3. I wish that 6-year-old Bobby Chew _____ .
4. When I was a child, my parents _____ .
5. This story makes me feel _____ .
6. Bobby Chew reminds me of _____ .
7. I _____ .

After you have completed the sentences above in your own way, you might wish to read some representative answers from my students.

One student writes;

1. Reading about this tragedy made me feel that one of the important things in life is for a child to have parents who care.
2. What hurts me most about this tragedy is that Bobby never knew the security of being loved by his parents regarding his condition.
3. I wish that 6-year-old Bobby could have known his parents *did* care.
4. When I was a child, my parents did care about me.
5. This story makes me feel very sad. My answer surprises me.
6. Bobby Chew reminds me of myself.
7. I cannot understand my sadness and its associations with me.

Another:

1. Reading about this tragedy made me feel that Bobby was a real little person, who carried on in spite of many difficulties. I am much impressed by some people's fortitude when faced with adversity, and wonder how I would react, faced with the same situation, or if I knew someone in that position. How do people (Bobby's "family") feel who can witness the buoyancy of such a child; how does it affect their lives?
2. What hurts me most about this tragedy is the relationship between Bobby's hospital family and his real parents. I mean, there must have been some bitterness on the part of the staff, first to know a child had been abandoned, and secondly that the parents would only reappear at the death of their child.
3. I wish that 6-year-old Bobby Chew could have realized just what he must have meant to all those around him. If he could have been an-

[1] *San José News,* January 21, 1970, p. 21.

gelic in the face of a great handicap, and eventually death, many must have cherished him a great deal. As a child, he may not have realized just what he was accomplishing in keeping his chin up.

4. When I was a child, my parents tried to protect me from all the bad things in the world. They taught me to be concerned with the welfare of others.
5. This story makes me feel angry because I am forced to feel pity.
6. Bobby Chew reminds me of all the rejected persons in the world.
7. I resent being forced into sentimentality.

A third student comments:

1. Reading about this tragedy made me feel that the responsibility of being a parent is great. And that happiness and inward peace may be attained through death. Everything happens for the best.
2. What hurts me most about this tragedy is Bobby never really had a chance! A chance to run, a chance to smile through clear eyes, just never had a chance to be, a chance to share his love, a chance to know his parents.
3. I wish that 6-year-old Bobby Chew could have been someone that I knew so that I could have learned to have that kind of courage in a world of despair.
4. When I was a child, my parents taught me to accept reality and that suffering is a part of life. My father's most famous quote from the Bible was "once an adult and twice a child." And in Bobby's case I think this was very true. First child stage at birth, the adult courage to face his problem with open eyes and the childlike qualities of being unable to explain why.
5. This story makes me feel mad at myself for not helping the underprivileged, the neglected, and the oppressed.
6. Bobby Chew reminds me of my own children.
7. I owe greater love and devotion to my own children.

Another:

1. Reading about this tragedy made me feel that parenthood or having children comes much too easy.
2. What hurts me most about this tragedy is parents of Bobby showing responsibility at his death.
3. I wish that 6-year-old Bobby Chew had never been born.
4. When I was a child, my parents shared the responsibility of raising me.
5. Some people ought to be sterilized, so that they cannot have children.
6. Bobby Chew reminds me of my own parents.
7. I am angry at his irresponsible parents.

And still another:

1. Reading about this tragedy made me feel that I was very depressed and didn't know what to do.
2. What hurts me most is that I don't have someone to go to for comfort.
3. I wish Bobby were a very little sneaky boy.
4. When I was a child my parents were always saving money for a rainy day.

Finally, a student writes:

1. Reading about this tragedy made me feel that the people who were concerned with his care and who attended the funeral could express only their own sense of loss which seems to me somehow futile. I would, had I been one of them, have hoped that I had made Bobby's life happy and meaningful while he was alive, rather than be concerned with the loss through his death.
2. What hurts most about this tragedy is that his parents could not face him while he was alive and only after his death did they appear which seems self-serving as was their initial abandonment of him.
3. I would wish 6-year-old Bobby Chew could have found fulfillment in his life even though it was shortened by his death and lacked the comfort of a real home and family.
4. When I was a child my parents were often gone or not available to me unless some type of crisis appeared imminent. My father was introverted and self-centered out of his fear of the world and my mother was usually too tired from work and dealing with her marital problems to relate to me except on a crisis basis. I think Bobby in many respects was fortunate with regards to the attention and caring he received.

This exercise was intended to let you have some insight into your capacity for suffering and your capacity for integrating pain. Above all, it was also an experiential effort to put you in touch with some truth about life through the pain of death. It is an excellent starter for an extended group discussion on the meaning of death.

I am going to suggest some additional exercises and fantasy experiences that can help you explore your feelings and discover personally how the beliefs and the anxieties about death lead to reverence and joy in life.

POSITIVE EXERCISES IN DEATH

There are many ways to help a person get in touch with the revealing and potentially healing dimension of his death. Some of the exercises I use are borrowed from psychologists Herman Feifel and Robert

Kastenbaum,[2] who have done a great deal of excellent work in this area.

In one such exercise, the subject is put into a mild trance and then asked to imagine that he is attending his own funeral. He is encouraged to develop that image extensively; he must think of himself visiting a funeral parlor and see himself lying in state, etc. Then he is urged to hear a friend talk honestly about him and what he had meant in life.

This exercise can be varied by suggesting that the subject, while still in a mild trance state, imagine that he has died and then come back to life again. This assists him in going through a rebirth fantasy. Such a guided experience can be very effective in clarifying the life-giving power of death.

Still another positive exercise is to write the script for your own death. It involves answering the question "How would you like to die?" Would you be rebellious? Would you rather be asleep? Do you want foreknowledge, or would you rather it is a surprise? Do you feel that you would be reconciled to your death? It helps to be as specific as possible in your answers.

A Question of When

I sometimes shock my freshman classes by asking them to write down the *age* at which they think they will die. It is important to write down a definite age and then think hard about why you selected it. That number puts your whole life in a new and strange perspective. And writing it down is the experience of commitment and of finality. In this threatening number a person is helped to discover who he is and who he is not, who he should be and who he should not be.

This simplest of exercises usually brings a strong reaction, especially from young people, who may have rarely reflected on their own death. The response often is a very distant age—99, 85, 72—some time far removed from the concrete reality of their present lives. Older people may give an age that is close to their present age. Middle-aged persons sometimes write down the age that is the end of their childbearing stage; these people seem to imagine death at an age at which their life is conceived to be half over. Sometimes the number indicates that for the subject the important part of his life is finished.

For example, if you are 30 and you say you are going to die at 60, you are really saying that your life is half over, and sometimes this

---

[2] Reported in personal conversations.

analysis can be a rather accurate picture of how you feel about your own life now. A 35-year-old woman writes down 48 as her age of death. Analysis shows that her youngest child is 6, so that at age 48 the child is 18 and leaves home. That is the time of death. Is she saying that without the children she is nothing?

When do you think *you* will die?

And then there is the question of probability. What is the probability that you will die now, tomorrow, in a year, ten years, in a quarter- or a half-century? Answering this question can get you in touch with this enormously potent phenomenon of your own death.

I occasionally conduct a marathon workshop on death. When people spend three long days dealing with this subject matter, they can become desensitized to death, and may find that death is a belief that is rather comfortable to live with. They often come to realize that the worry about death is an artificial one, one that is culturally learned. Finally, the marathon can sometimes help people gain a sense of peace and comfort from an acceptance of their own mortality.

A Question of How

There are other related exercises you can do to come to grips with your own death. For instance, *where* do you think you will die? What will you be doing? Will you die in a hospital? At home? On the street? Is death something that will come to you from the outside, or from the inside? You may have difficulty answering because of course you do not know. However, you should get in touch with your intuitive mechanism. Will death come from behind? From in front? From above, or below? These questions put you in touch with the full knowledge that you are a dying being, and that you start dying the moment you are born. Jung was right when he wrote in his introduction to the translation of *The Tibetan Book of the Dead* that the diagnosis for "good health" is "mortal illness," because that condition always ends in death. The prognosis of good health is death. Man is mortally stricken with life. Life leads inevitably to death.

A young mother in one of my encounter groups on death told the group tearfully that she had finally been able to do something she had always wanted to do, and that was to tell her father, with whom she had had a bad relationship, that she loved him.

By using exercises like the ones described in this chapter, it is possible to make powerful discoveries by the courageous facing of the reality of your own death.

9

Death and Values

Awareness of death clarifies our values. As a result, death can give meaning to life.

RETROACTIVE MEANING OF LIFE

Through the knowledge that death is inevitable, that death *is* a reality to you, your life can be given meaning retroactively. The fact that you exist now, have existed in the past, and have built up a life for yourself, are realities to cherish, regardless of who you are and what you have achieved. You will become better able to prize, respect, and revere yourself when you face the fact of your own death in the future.

All life—including life that is past—is too precious and sacred to be denigrated. Life, vis-a-vis death, is holy. You can't reject it, and you should not have contempt for it, even if you may feel guilt about your past. And is the past really as bad as we think it is? In fact, is your life as ineffective, unaccomplished, unfulfilled as you may think it is? To be able to find meaning in your past life can be supremely calming and reassuring. If you face the fact that you will die, that your life is indeed limited, what has already transpired will be made more precious, more valuable, more sacred. You will be able to understand your uniqueness and the fact that *you are irreplaceable.* What is past is exactly as unique as what is now and what will be. What is past is as irreplaceable as what will be. With death in the future your past becomes a work of art. The sculpture that was in the attic turns out to be an original Michaelangelo. The sculpture has not changed, but you now recognize its great value. You may own a Picasso drawing of a certain value. But Picasso has died; there will be no more drawings, ever. Your drawing, without having changed, is enhanced in value. That is how your past can be experienced, if you accept the reality of death.

However, many people complain about their wasted past, often fearing that they will not be able to grow because they cannot confront the grief of having "messed up" their past. They need desperately to face and deal with this grief.

Grief Work

This point is referred to in existential therapy, especially by J. F. T. Bugental, as "grief work." The longer you wait and the older you get, the more difficult it becomes to change. Why? Because with change comes the admission that your past life may have been a mistake. In this connection the principle of retroactive meaning is invaluable. Once in touch with grief and regret about your past, you discover that it contains substance and value. You discover that part of you *is* a fine person. Regardless of how depressed you may be about the life gone by, your past has not been a total loss. On the contrary, if you have been confronted with terrible odds, with insidious rejection, then look how magnificently you rose to the occasion; how nobly you have rescued yourself from this quagmire. Observe your present strength, your capacity for survival, your power to give meaning to your life. Remember: it might have been easier to give up! This attitude is part of grief work—it enables you to begin to develop the sense that your life has indeed had meaning. This is retroactive meaning.

This point leads to another illustration. Let us say that there are many valuable original Michelangelo sculptures. One day all but one are destroyed. The remaining one has not changed—but it has now asumed much greater value than before.

And so it is with you. Your past has not changed. But its importance and meaning can change greatly once you realize that because death exists your past is irreplaceable; it exists uniquely, only once. It is yours. It is you.

PROACTIVE MEANING OF LIFE

Your confrontation of your own death can also give meaning to the future. The very knowledge that you will die can give you courage and integrity. You gain the ability to rely on your capacity to define yourself, to assign values to yourself, to be your own monitor, judge, validator—all of which are hallmarks of maturity. You can live by *your own values*. You cannot be and do everything, changing direction with the wind. The decision of where you are going in life is yours alone to make, and you must do so comfortably. That decision establishes your identity and helps you live your life with the integrity and courage necessary to be yourself.

Our pluralistic society gives us endless messages about "right" values—but we must select our own. Because our world does not give us a single or uniform message about true values, we are forced to invent our own. And in this necessity lies both the individualizing strength and the anxiety-producing weakness of contemporary society. You find it possible to choose your own values only if you know that this life is "it": you will die your own death; no one will do it for you. Therefore, *you* must make the courageous self-definitions, the decisions about your life.

INTIMACY

A further insight to be gained from facing our own death is that of the great value of intimacy. When you take death seriously, the distant future is transformed into the now. This pressures you to make intimacy real, to risk intimacy *now* instead of waiting for some moment in the future.

Knowing about death leads to a greater need and possibility for intimacy partly because death is a very lonely experience. Intimacy is the sharing of loneliness, and through sharing such a need we become more fully ourselves.

One of the most useful metaphors for consciousness is God. To the extent that consciousness emphasizes its potential for the cosmic and the universal, it is also very lonely. Only by limiting itself—through death—can loneliness be overcome. The more we penetrate the inner recesses of our consciousness, the closer we get to God and the more we learn about loneliness.

God is very much alone because it is logically impossible for this omnipotent being to create another such being. Try to imagine such vast loneliness and you may be able to grasp more fully the tragedy of aloneness. The person who does not understand this, one whom you might call the perennial extrovert, may well be less capable of genuine and profound intimacy than the person who has known loneliness.

What is more intimate than the sharing of loneliness? Is it possible for a person to appreciate intimacy if he has never plumbed the depths of loneliness? Imagine a person who is not alone, who does not feel alone, who does not recognize the loneliness of his inward consciousness or his "transcendental ego," the aloneness of the Eternal Now. Does he know intimacy?

The aloneness of our individual consciousness demonstrates the value of intimacy. But intimacy can be achieved only if we limit ourselves and respect the absolute reality of another.

EGO-TRANSCENDING ACHIEVEMENT

In addition to giving life meaning retroactively, proactively, and in relation to intimacy, there is another value to be gained from confronting death. This is the realization of the extroverted need for ego-transcending achievement. An authentic person is not only self-centered, and passionately concerned with his inwardness, but he is also equally concerned with the outside world. When focused outward, he experiences a kind of ego loss. Whereas the importance of intimacy, and meaning for the past and the future have their roots in inwardness or introspection, the motivation for ego-transcending achievements is grounded in a focus on the outside world, the future, and in general on that which is distant. The authentic person has a need to make a meaningful contribution to the lives of others. I believe that human beings are *not* basically selfish.

Let me illustrate. Some people feel that the goal of doing a job is to be paid for it; that the value is not in *doing* the job but in the paycheck after it is done. But I do not believe that most people are this insensitive and egocentric. The arrogant self-concern that is often said to be associated with a capitalist system is, in my opinion, culturally imposed. It is true that there will always be those who think that only idiots selflessly contribute to society. But for the many who know they will die, the emptiness of this egocentrism, the hollowness of being selfish on principle, is apparent. Being useful to others can be one of the greatest meaning-giving aspects of your life. By making a contribution that transcends your life you are saying that there is something in this world more important than you.

The value of ego-transcending actions cannot be culturally taught; it is not an acquired trait. It emerges directly from the innermost nature of the person. Even if you were taught to be selfish, there will come a time—when you ultimately have to face death—when you will realize that doing something for others does have value. It feels good; it feels right. The desire to make a contribution exists, which implies that people are good, decent, responsive, friendly, kind, trustworthy, and capable of love.

The authentic person thus finds his meaning in making a contribution, in giving. When you are confronted with death you become aware of the need for ego-transcending achievement. So knowledge of your own death can teach you that *giving* is an important value.

Many people have very low opinions of themselves. As a result they also have low opinions of others and expect others to return such feelings. In fact, a person's lack of regard for others may be a way of "getting even" with them for their presumably similar sentiments. It is easy to see how an unwillingness to contribute to society can be a result of this vicious cycle.

The consequent philosophic-therapeutic question is this: How can such a person develop a high self-esteem? How can he be helped to achieve self-confidence, ego strength, integrity? The answer, I believe, lies in his honest exploration of the reality that death is in the future. Facing this awesome and certain fact, in giving meaning to the life of the past and the future, and in making intimacy possible, can enable a person to acquire strength and dignity and worth.

Let us now explore some practical and therapeutic applications of these insights.

George W.

George W. was a man in his early thirties, and was married with no children. He was one of nine children. He did not have any specific complaints, but he insisted he was very unhappy. He had what appears to be an excellent marriage—and he wanted out, but he didn't know why. The only reason he gave was that his wife was too good for him. That is an unusual reason for a divorce, one that has not yet been incorporated into the legal structure: incompatibility on the grounds that "she is good and I am bad." George stressed that he thought the world of his wife; she was marvelous in every respect, but he did not feel at ease with her. Moreover, he was having an affair. He was eager to talk to me, even though he was not clear about what he wanted. I asked if he wanted me to help him break off with his wife or to make up with her. He simply couldn't answer this. I therefore used a device to break an impasse, to engender movement in the philosophic counseling situation. That device is based on this existential principle of freedom and responsibility: You are subjectively responsible for your perception of your world; that is to say, your world reflects your choices and your self-image.

"I Am"

I told George that if he should succeed in achieving what he wanted out of our meetings—even though at the time he did not know what these goals were—he would in effect be saying to himself, *I am, I exist.* In other words, his way of affirming himself was to achieve something important to him from our meetings. That is how he would be able to express a conviction that he exists. However, if in his own eyes he failed in our meetings by not achieving anything of value to him, he would be saying to himself, *I do not exist, I am nothing.* His manner of expressing the fact that he is nothing at all—that he does not exist, that he *is not*, that he is in fact suicidal—would be borne out if he achieved nothing in our meetings.

To the extent that he had so far been unable to formulate anything meaningful in our meetings, he was indeed failing. Something had impelled him to come, but he was not willing to discover what it was. I believe that such mirroring of responsibility is very important. It is not enough for a person to seek help by saying, "Here I am, now make me better." Although the counselor must assume responsibility in his own mind for the success of the philosophic counseling, he cannot share that knowledge with his client. As far as his client is concerned, he himself is expected to assume complete responsibility for creating meaning in his life. Thus, when the therapist communicates this expectation to his patient, a device is created that will help in bringing about a sense of responsibility, and thereby a way will open up for the patient to begin to see meaning in his life.

Commitment

Another way used to break the impasse was to point out to George that his commitment to our meetings—the seriousness with which he approached them and the amount of work he was willing to do in them—would be measures of his commitment to *his own personal growth.* I told him, "These meetings are your time and are devoted exclusively to you. Therefore, if you make a commitment to them and show an ability and a willingness to really work, then you are in fact expressing a commitment to yourself."

This attitude may make a client feel guilty, and even angry, because it makes it appear as if the counselor were passing the buck to cover his own incompetence. But these considerations are irrelevant, because there is no time in a counseling hour to discuss the merits of the advisor. During that period the complete effort goes to serve the client's needs. And in order to achieve maximum effectiveness, the counselor must make clear to the patient that understanding and solving his own problem is *his* responsibility.

Retroactive Meaning

It soon became apparent that George's real problem had nothing to do with his wife, his mistress, or his marriage. The problem was within himself, and the key issue was a question of assigning meaning to his life retroactively.

He expressed a thought that carried within it a tremendous amount of affect: he believed he had been cheated out of his childhood. That hurts! If you adopt the view that you are the product of your childhood and believe that you have been cheated of that childhood, then your situation is indeed troubled. From that nonexistential point of view, your childhood is a *fait accompli*; it is part of the unchangeable closed past. Only a philosophy of freedom, which shows you that you can change retroactively the meaning of your past, can enable a person to overcome this grief. And we had to make that option a living one for George.

The Middle Child

George was the middle child in a large family, and I believe that an important determiner of a person's character or personality is his position among siblings. The middle child is sometimes forgotton or overlooked; the prominent places seem to be the first and last.[1] That is why I said to George that to the extent that he made progress in our meetings, he would not feel overlooked any more. And to the extent that he did not make progress, he would still perceive himself as being the same overlooked person: an individual who does not exist, who *is not*. In other words, I set about to help him reconstruct his past so that he could ultimately say, "I am important and recognized." When George told me that he was the middle child, I suspected that

[1] Sometimes, in large families, a second child will be the first child in a cluster of children who are close together, or he will be a last child for a while. Whereas technically he is a middle child, practically he can be a first or a last child.

he did not have any strong concept of his own existence and identity. Then I told him that his success in our meetings would be proof of the fact that "you feel real, that you have an identity," whereas their failure would prove that he does not in fact have an identity. I related the story of a family with eight children. Several years ago the family had gone to the beach and accidentally left one of the children, a 4-year-old, there. When they returned to the city they discovered that the little fellow was missing. They quickly drove back—and there he was, still sitting and playing on the beach, very much adapted to his situation.

George was touched rather deeply by this story; because he himself had felt equally overlooked all his life. No one had ever seemed to know the difference if he was missing. No one seemed to care. He then told me how as a child he would often try to run away and hide to make the family aware of his existence through his absence. But no one missed him; they didn't even know that he had run away. There was no way he could call attention to himself. He could not coerce the world into validating his existence, his individuality, or his identity. I asked him, "Would you have preferred to be an only child?" He cried, and said, "Yes, yes."

His family experiences taught him that he was not real, that he did not exist. And to compound the insult of having been overlooked in his childhood, it turned out that he had been born on his father's birthday. He suffered the same fate as a child born on Christmas day, who may never have a decent birthday celebration of his own. Furthermore, George's father was too busy for him, as one can well understand. He had had no decent education and held only a poor job; he had great difficulties supporting his large family. Because his father never did anything with him, George resented him. And it became my responsibility to convince him that in our meetings he was going to learn that he does exist, that he was indeed real, and has always *been* an individual identity. I continued, "To the extent that you begin to feel that you are real, you are making progress, but to the extent that you continue to feel that you do not exist, you are not making any progress at all." In this gentle manner I tried to force contact with reality, to bring about a grip on life.

Add it all up, and you have a person who recognized, painfully, that he was blocking out everthing in his life before the age of eight because he felt he hadn't even existed as a person. It was my responsibility to convince him that he *was* real, and that he had always *had* an individual identity.

How to Find Meaning

How was George to find meaning in his life? He needed to assign meaning to his life retroactively; therefore, I made the following suggestions based on an existential approach to mental health. First, I reassured him that his pain was very important. It was, in fact, the one aspect of his life—and of his past—that indicated that he was not being cheated at that moment. His pain was proof of contact with his reality, with the stream of life, both present and past. As long as he could weep over his lost childhood, he was in touch with its reality. Therefore he still owned a childhood; it was not, after all, lost. Weeping over his lost childhood may have been a childish thing to do, because in effect that made him again a child who is not being recognized as such. His pain was his real contact with his actual childhood. Knowledge of this fact would enable him to recover that childhood.

If on the other hand he had felt no pain, I explained, then all contact would have been severed; he would not have felt that he had been cheated out of his childhood, and then the problem of assigning meaning to his life retroactively would not have arisen.

Such pain is therapeutic because it is the experience of the point of contact. George's pain was the pain of a child, frustrated, rejected, and unloved. And to the degree that he acted like a child in mourning the missing childhood, he was in touch with his childhood.

Second, I assured George that a person who *survives* any difficult period in his life with emotional balance has grounds to be proud of himself. Unfortunately, the reverse is often the case. A person like George will feel guilty about his lost childhood. Someone who has gone through traumatic experiences in his life is likely to feel inadequate precisely because of these experiences, and yet in truth the exact opposite is the case. It is possible for a person who has managed to survive a traumatic time to be more authentic, more mature, more adaptable, stronger and healthier than a person who has not met the test of fire. This insight needs to be worked through in the lives of most persons, especially those who have gone through a troublesome and difficult past. They need to see that through the disadvantages they have survived they have learned strength and courage.

We now reach a point at which we can understand that there are two ways by which a person can choose to give meaning to his life retroactively. One is by feeling a sense of tragedy about his childhood. This tells him that he has a second chance, because he is a child all over again right now. The past is no longer closed. Another is a decision to perceive the unfortunate past as a mistake, and to more accurately appraise it with respect and gratitude for what it has made possible.

A Feeling of Importance

People tend to feel guilty and inadequate about a deprived past; they are taught to believe this way by their peers. It all starts in childhood. For example, when a child has a parent who is dead, he is often ridiculed by other children. The child may then react by saying to himself, "There must be something wrong with me; there is a defect in me." A dead parent is like a missing finger or limb: the affected child will tend to feel self-conscious and as a result feel less worthy than others.

I had the understanding with George that I would not see his wife, just him. Why? He had put his wife on a pedestal; his relationship with her was a manifestation of his basic premise that he himself did not in fact exist as an individual identity. He was not important. His wife, however, *was* important; in his perception of the world she *did* exist. I underscored to him that for me he was the most important one; I wanted to talk only to him. He liked that. It was a way of saying that ours was a relationship for him only. I was making it impossible for him to set up a situation in which he and his wife would come in and the relationship would then be dominated by his wife's needs. That helped George.

The Most Important and Difficult
Retroactive Meaning

The third way of helping George develop meaning to his life retroactively was the most important, but it was also the most difficult to achieve. I asked George, knowing in advance his answer, whether he and his wife planned to have children. He said no. A person who has rejected his own childhood, who feels that it never existed, would not be interested in creating a new child. The point, on which we worked for a long time, was that the most meaningful way in which he could recreate his own lost childhood, redefine himself as a person with a childhood, and in general redefine to himself the meaning of being a child, was by dealing with and committing himself to a child. This was not to say, "Have a child and then your problems will be over";—that would have been false and cruel. But for George I felt that only through a commitment to a real living child, a child that would be as dependent on him as he had been on his parents, would he be able to relive and then reconstruct his own childhood. He would accomplish this not vicariously, through abreactions and fantasies, but directly, through a living person and a real relationship. And again, the measure of his success in recreating his *own* childhood was to be how good a father figure he would be to a *real* child.

He started out on this proposed program by joining the Big Brother organization. He made a year's contractual commitment to a young boy. This was an intelligent, rational way of handling the problem of intimacy with his own childhood. No new person was created and a social need was fulfilled. As George developed closeness with his boy, he changed his perceptions of his own childhood. The fact that he himself did not go fishing with his father ceased to pain him when he went fishing with this boy. George's relationship with the child gave a new meaning to a past that he had thought was closed. But the emotional tone of it was not closed and for George it was reconstructed.

Ultimately, George became a splendid and responsible Big Brother. Soon thereafter his wife became pregnant; my relationship with him terminated when the child was born. He was then ready to be a loving father. The Big Brother program helped him to rebuild the meaning of his past. As a result, his present and future changed dramatically.

We say in psychology that your past creates you, determines you, but we forgot to say, with philosophy, that *you can change the emotional meaning of that past*. That your past creates you remains true, but now a different, reconstructed past creates for you a better life. By changing your perceptions of your own childhood, your past will be changed emotionally. As a result, the present person that the new past creates will be different: he will be loving, warm, and accepting because he has acquired self-respect.

The case of George illustrates the possibility and significance of assigning meanings retroactively.

Before concluding this chapter we should describe briefly a helpful exercise for helping people to achieve retroactive meaning.

AUTOBIOGRAPHY EXERCISE

A useful way to help an individual give meaning to his life retroactively is by having him write his autobiography. This should not be simply a chronological recounting but rather an emphasis on some of the following points:

1. *For whom are you writing this autobiography?* Some older people wish to dedicate it to their children, as a gesture through which they show them who their parents were. It is a final and deep expression of love toward the children; it settles a great deal of unfinished business.

2. *How did you come to lead the life that in fact you did?* This kind of analysis can help a person view himself with a great deal of love, understanding, and compassion.

3. *What can you teach others through your own experiences?* This topic tends to give value to experience that may have passed unnoticed.

4. *What do you now know about yourself?* The writing of an autobiography is a beautiful act of self-affirmation; it is a highly effective way of saying "I am."

5. *What are the implications for the future?* Often, the writing of an autobiography gives present and future meaning to a person's life, regardless of age, because it sets new goals.

This exercise is useful for all ages. It is easy, effective, interesting, and in general a very pleasant experience.

We now move to the crucial existential issue of taking personal responsibility for our own private death. That discussion puts us in touch with the deeper regions of our unconscious and with the important mysteries of our decision-making processes.

10

We Invent Death

DEATH IS AN INVENTION

I insist that death is an invention, and I shall attempt to explain that view.

One student responded to this assertion as follows: "Since we may have invented death and birth, both inexperienceable, why then do we presume that we are condemned to die? Why do we choose to believe that life is an incurable disease and that our mortality is coeval with nothingness?"

What the student has done here is to call attention to a rather obvious contradiction. I, as a phenomenologist and existentialist, say that death is inevitable and on the other hand, as an empiricist (that is, a scientist for whom truth rests on observation), I say that death is an invention. We invent death in that we decide whether or not to identify with the stream of the cosmos or separate from it.

If we delete from our experience all assumptions and constructs, then we see before us what the philosopher calls pure and undiluted reality. That primordial reality does not contain within it the concept of the individual. The ideas that there exists an ego and that I am that ego are not, strictly speaking, given to us as presuppositionless data in experience. They are constructed out of the raw material of sensations and emotions that the world gives us. As an infant, I do not think of myself as an ego; nor do I feel separate from the world. I *learn* to think of myself as an ego and to think of the world as different from me. Language helps teach me that, since all sentences are split into subject and object.

It is my contention, which I realize is controversial, that the basic way to construct the sense that I am an ego which is different from the world is through the concept of death. Death is a word, an idea, and even an image. If I accept that image as real (and without proof, strictly speaking), it produces the feeling that I am an ego. In that sense I can say that death is invented, that I am responsible for death, and that death is the clue to an understanding of the nature of individuality. I have never experienced myself being dead. But I *have* experienced myself being anxious about the possibility of being dead in the future. That feeling is in fact the feeling of being an individual. And because I have no proof for the death-of-myself, it is clear that I *accept* the death-of-myself in a free act of belief. In that sense I invent my death. More on this later.

Let us explore at this point the implications of the fact that my death is never experienced by me. In this book we are not talking about the *experience* of death. There is no such thing. We talk about the *anticipation* of death. That is all we have. *Death is an invention which we need in order to feel alive.* The same truth applies to birth. No one has experienced either his birth or his conception. These beliefs about the origin and destiny of our inmost subjectivity are all theories; they are not facts based on personal experience. The birth-of-myself, as well as the death-of-myself are metaphysical concepts of the order of God, substance, infinity, subatomic particles, the reality of other minds, electromagnetic waves, etc. We are convinced of the reality of our absolute limits—death and birth—yet neither of them can be experienced even in principle. That is a simple and basic fact worthy of reflection. It is based on a sensitive description and analysis of our immediate experience, whose data are the foundation of all knowledge. It is also a point of intensely dramatic consequences.

Empiricism

Let me be more specific with this important point. In an empirically oriented philosophy—a philosophy that says we must accept only what is actually experienced—and in a philosophy that makes a qualitative distinction between the death-of-myself and the death-of-another, an extraordinary phenomenon occurs. It is true that I can experience the death of *another* and I can experience the birth of *another*. But I am now interested in understanding the birth and death of *myself.* The birth and death of the inward subjectivity that I call *myself* are different from the birth and death of that entity I call *another.* The reason is that a "me" or a "myself" is a subject, whereas a "you" or an "other" is an object. I, the subject, can never become the object of my perception or my understanding. Conversely, any object can never be said to have the properties of being the subject that I experience myself to be. As a result we can never argue from the nature of an object to that of a subject. Therefore I cannot infer the reality of my own death from observing the death of another; nor can I infer my own birth from my observation of the birth of another. To argue about the nature of the subject in a field of consciousness from what we observe in the object of that field (you have died, therefore I will die) is logically invalid. We would have to assume the identity of inequalities. It is like arguing from oranges to bananas.

Types

These are different types of events. "The other" is in the realm of the object. "I" am in the realm of the subject. I am the only subjectivity I will ever know. I know endless numbers of objects. If I am going to make statements about the nature of my *subjectivity*, I cannot infer anything about its structure from a point of view that depends on *objectivity*. Therefore, I am confronted, as an empiricist, with this bizarre situation—that the two cardinal poles of my subjective existence, my birth and my death, are beyond my experience; in fact, they are forever beyond my experience.

The fact that I cannot argue from a condition of objects (i.e., the birth of another and the death of another) to a condition of subjectivity is a "category mistake"—or a confusion of "types" (borrowing terms from Gilbert Ryle and Bertrand Russell).

The entire theory of knowledge that follows from phenomenological explorations, especially what is called the *theory of the intentionality of consciousness*, makes it clear that to infer about a structure in the inmost ego (the transcendental region, the region of the field of consciousness that is forever the observer and cannot be observed) from what we perceive to be the case in the realm of objects (the empirical realm) is without any warrant whatsoever. To argue from the death of another to my death, from your death to my death, or, more precisely, from the death of the objects of consciousness to the death of that consciousness itself, is a form of argumentation that lacks all conceivable justification.

If I had to make a commitment, which is rather difficult to do in such esoteric matters, I would say that death is not real, it *is* an invention. In fact, it is not even a hypothesis, because logic does not permit us to argue even hypothetically from the realm of objects to the transcendental realm of conscious subjectivity. There is a further point.

Deception

One core aspect of our invention of death is to deceive ourselves into believing it is not an invention or a game but that it is reality. We invent death so that then we can take it with utmost seriousness. We invent the game of dying in order to play it for real. And when we play it, part of the rules of the game are that we forget that these are rules; we accept them as reality. So there is in human existence a certain amount of ambiguity, a kind of irony: we lead a two-tier existence. At the heart of this self-deception is the rejection of our nature as a transcendental consciousness. This self-deception is the act of full embodiment; it is the phenomenon of individuation. Forgetting our transcendental nature, deceiving ourselves about our own deathlessness—or, better said, the deathlessness that runs through us—is the very metaphysical act which creates us as individuals. Self-deception of this type is humanity-creating. Let us examine this important point a bit further.

RESPONSIBILITY FOR BEING HUMAN

With the invention of death we have invented the human being. By inventing death, by creating and accepting death, we have also invented finitude; and finitude is limitation and is thus the principle of individuation. When we say, "I will die," we are thereby saying "I am *different* from the rest of the world because the world will go on when I can no longer. Death is the experience of opposition because it occurs against my will. Death is like a foreign body in my system. I am isolated, insulated, separate from the rest of the world." And by separating myself in that way, by experiencing myself not as coterminus with nature, *not as one* with nature or with a cosmos, but as *isolated*, different from the cosmos—namely, individual—I have created myself as a person and I have created the sense of my own identity, the sense of my own individuality.

There is an important humanizing and therapeutic corollary to this view. Once I fully understand that my ego, my individuality, is really my own invention, if I understand that experientially as well as intellectually, something of extraordinary importance happens. At that moment I assume full, total, uncompromising, and unequivocal responsibility for my existence! I finally understand the meaning of responsibility, of freedom, the existential point that I am indeed in charge of my life.

When I integrate into my being the insight that consciousness invents individuality by expressing that creative act through the belief in the certainty of death, then I can say with conviction, "I am my own creator; I am responsible for what and who I am." And at that moment a person fully comprehends the well-known statement found on President Truman's desk that read, "The buck stops here." Here, where I am, is the end of the line. *Here* the decisions will be made. I assume full responsibility. This insight made Truman into the kind of person who had the courage to develop the Marshall Plan, who—rightly or wrongly—could drop the first atomic bomb, and who made many other decisions that were difficult and courageous. It was because of his belief that "the buck stops here" that he could take full responsibility for what he was and did.

The moment I recognize that I create myself through death, I assume full responsibility for my limitations and for my finitude. It is also true that our complaints about life are related to our finitude. What is the answer to our finitude? If there is an answer, it is, "I assume full, total, complete and personal charge of my finitude."

I believe that this is the basic nature of individuality; it is essential to understand this if counseling and psychotherapy are to work. Let us now examine some implications of this view.

DO WE SECRETLY WANT WHAT TROUBLES US MOST?

Death, our greatest trouble, may in the end be also a secret wish. One message of the view that we invent death is that we must assume responsibility for our finitude, as we have seen. From this we can posit a theory that the things that trouble us deeply may also be, in some mysterious way, the things that we really want. Such a belief, if it is true, would solve most of our problems; consequently we must guard ourselves against wishful thinking, rationalization, and fantasy.

There are several ways of illustrating this hypothesis at the experiential level. For example, answer for yourself the question, "What troubles me most?" Focus and condense that answer in some succinct form—a sentence, an image, or a concept. Now try the impossible, the outrageous—persuade yourself that what troubles you most deeply is really what you secretly want the most. It is this type of guided daydream that will help you take responsibility for your pain. I have found that one way of modifying the empirical ego through the spoken word is by using the technique of a good, well-trained orator or singer: use your diaphragm, give your voice support; feel that the base of your lungs and your stomach support your voice. Your voice must rise from the base of your being, symbolized by the pelvic region, and not just from the upper portions of your torso. Now, speaking in this way, construct a sentence that says in effect, "I want my troubles!" What may happen is that the act of freely choosing that negation will surface to the level of consciousness. At that moment you may experience that *what you desire most intensely,* and therefore choose, *is* in fact the very existence of this final frustration, the final *proof of your finitude.*

The second device that I have found useful in modifying, changing, reorganizing someone's mode of perception is to ask that he listen carefully to his own voice. In this exercise, do not identify with your voice, merely *listen* to it. Hear it as if it were coming from some place outside you. As you step back from attachment to your voice you *are not* you empirical ego, but you *perceive* your empirical ego. If you say, "I, (————) want, desire, love, demand that which troubles me most," it is conceivable that you will perhaps perceive your whole world in an entirely new, different, and fresh way. Certainly the idea is worth some experimentation. It is obvious that much of philosophy and religion have tried to accomplish this transformation, as has art. Experiment with yourself and see what unexpected possibilities may develop for you.

DEATH AS SELF-WILLED

There are two more points to be made to help clarify the hypothesis that death is invented. The atavistic view that finitude is self-willed and that therefore suffering is a necessary part of a larger good has been too often in the past used for tyrannical social control. Any conservative government can use this philosophy to prevent change.

A student of mine stated this point very well when he wrote, "The need to control numerous pawns by the few of royal blood requires perpetuation of a myth. There is a higher meaning in suffering, in the life hereafter: be a slave now and sup later!"

Ideas can be misused, just as medical, pharmacological, chemical, or nuclear knowledge can be misused. The fact that the knowledge that brought about the peaceful uses of atomic energy has been misused in bombs is not logically related to the truth or falsity of that knowledge.

The same applies to the important hypothesis that death and finitude can be perceived as self-willed. The fact that this idea can be misused and put into the service of human tyranny is not logically related to its truth.

Life without suffering (i.e., without death and finitude) is without any meaning. But to hold this view is not to justify evil, nor is it to accept pain. On the contrary, this view gives us the strength to redouble the power with which we attack evil.

Even if utopia were ever achieved on this earth, there would still remain enough suffering to make a devoted philosophical analysis and response to it an inescapable necessity. We are therefore confronted with the ultimate philosophic issue: Can there be life without suffering? Is life that does not have suffering in it really life? The answer to these questions is a clear "no"; there can be no life without suffering. Suffering is the negative aspect of life, needed either to create a sense of individuality and with it a sense of being human, or to overcome the experience of finitude and thus bring about the sense of the divine in man.

ISOLATION OR AT ONE WITH NATURE?

The following objection from a medical student is a common criticism of the existential emphasis on individuality-through-death. He says, "Death is natural; it is part of the cycle of physiology and evolution, part of the cycle of the seasons and of reproduction. We need not overdramatize death." He feels that in truth he is an organism and that birth and death are phenomena of equal reality and meaning for him. I must respond thus: "If this view of death as natural is of some succor to you—if you can accept the view that you are part of the stream of nature and your fate is the fate of nature—then well and good. If you see yourself as part of the flow and balance of nature then you will not be perturbed by the fact that you have been condemned to die."

Nevertheless, the soothing view that death is natural makes sense only if you identify yourself with all of nature or with the cosmic stream of consciousness. And this point is the essence of the present analysis of death: We are individuals only to the extent that we are separated from the spatio-temporal infinity that envelops us. Self-affirmation—that is, affirmation of our individuality—is brought about by no-saying to our environment. And it is not soothing to define yourself as an alienated and isolated individual. What soothes is the *universality*.

Let me be specific. If you do not balance the temporal and the eternal—if you choose to recognize only the cosmic—you believe that you are a consciousness that is neither born nor will die. You consider yourself a consciousness that is part of a cosmic consciousness, like the empty space-time that pervades the universe, and in this case you have already overcome death. Why? Because when you sense the cosmic consciousness that runs through you, then you have given up this invention that is called death and with it you have given up individuality—this image that is called the person. Under those circumstances, you are certainly not anxious about death. But the price you pay for cosmic consciousnes is the loss of the sense of individuality.

Similarly, if you think of yourself, as the doctor did, as a body that is a continuous part of the flow of natural events, you have again overcome your individuality. At that moment you identify with all of nature. You may think longingly of the ideals of the Sierra Club and the poetry and essays of Emerson and Thoreau. Through these ideals, identification with the cosmos occurs not on the level of pure consciousness but on the level of material substance or nature.

We of course are part of the stream of nature, but if we identify ourselves totally with nature, we are no longer individuals. And it is the individual that is created by the phenomenon of death.

The existential concepts that must be invoked here are two: the two egos (the transcendental and empirical) and the theory of the intentionality of consciousness. With respect to the first, I must recognize that I am part of the cosmic space-time consciousness stream at the same time I am an isolated, finite individual. And with respect to the second, I discover that the sense of unity with being can occur regardless of whether I identify with and focus on the subjective realm (in which case I am a cosmic consciousness) or relate myself to the objective realm of being (in which case I am part of the stream of evolution, life, and nature).

When we accept death as a terrifying prospect, then, by virtue of that terror, we also define ourselves as individuals. However, if we do not accept death as terrifying, but as natural, then we have by that act merged with the stream of nature or of cosmic space-time consciousness. In the latter case, we will then not think seriously about the threat of death.

I must underscore once more that choosing to be individual or to be cosmic (either as empty space-time consciousness or as material-evolving nature) are both altogether authentic possibilities of our actual, experienced existence. That is part of the dialectical reasoning in back of these existential analyses.

If it is true that we invent our own death, it certainly follows that we must confront squarely the sensitive issue of suicide. To that point we now turn.

11

Suicide

IS IT MORAL?

Any philosophic analysis of death must sooner or later confront the issue of suicide. If we deal honestly with suicide, we must necessarily explore some rather dangerous and unpleasant possibilities. For one, we must re-examine our common assumption that suicide is bad and is to be prevented at all costs. The person who sets about to kill himself may feel that this is a difficult but perfectly sensible answer to a problem that has no other solution. We must be ready to entertain the thought that the decision for suicide is a choice fully within the province of human freedom and that it can have the character of authenticity. We must admit the possibility that under some circumstances suicide is the proper and ethical action. No therapist or friend is legally permitted to explore with an individual the possibility of authentic suicide, because in our society that can be interpreted as encouragement. I am in full agreement with that legal concept: we have the obligation to save lives. But seen from a philosophical perspective, suicide may in some cases represent a personal choice based on moral grounds. Encouraging suicide is totally immoral; we must nevertheless recognize that freedom for suicide is one of our civil liberties.

We define political liberty by saying that each person has a complete right over his own life, dominion over his body, control over his empirical ego. And if it is his decision to end it all (assuming sanity), if it is his considered judgment that the right action is to kill himself, then should not we respect his freedom of self-definition? Percy Bridgman, the Nobel Laureate physicist, committed suicide, when he was old and incurably ill. In his final note he said that today may be the last day he can end his life. Would it have been right to make him spend another three or four months in unbearable suffering? Closely related to such concerns is the legality of euthanasia: provisions may have to be made for legal suicide in certain cases.

How can a philosopher or therapist engaged in existential analysis, or in existential depth psychotherapy, discuss the issue of suicide with his patient? An existential counselor must respect totally the complete freedom of his patient at all times. But when the discussion turns to suicide, the therapist is not allowed to be completely open with his patient. He can no longer reflect the authentic inwardness of his patient. Instead, the therapist must manipulate his patient into a life-affirming rather than life-denying behavior system, regardless of what the integrity of the patient in fact demands. The therapist is told by his conscience, his system of ethics, and by the legal interpretation, "You must steer the patient, persuade him, even trick him or force him into choosing life." The same holds true of marriage counseling: the first obligation of the therapist is to save the marriage. The purpose is noble but the approach is anti-existential because it preempts the absolute freedom of the patient. However, as soon as a person feels manipulated or tricked, the sacred relationship of witness, trust, and encounter between therapist and patient is disrupted. And then the patient loses his trust and confidence. A *totally* open existential therapeutic relationship must make room for everything, including suicide. Only in such a way can the freedom of the patient be recognized and nurtured. Otherwise the therapeutic relationship is a partial one only. Unless a therapist permits himself to witness his patient's free choice of death, he cannot witness his choice of life. And a life that cannot choose itself as a life is not an authentic life. The choice here is between an authentic life and no life at all. There exists no compromise, unfortunately. The unwillingness to admit the possibility of authentic suicide severely truncates the effectiveness of a psychotherapeutic relationship.

Let us examine an actual suicide.

THE SUICIDE OF SERGEANT KAVANAUGH, EX-POW

According to newspaper articles at the time, the events leading up to young Kavanaugh's suicide unfolded in the following manner.

While serving with the Marines in South Vietnam, Sergeant Abel Larry Kavanaugh was captured on April 24, 1968, by the enemy and held prisoner almost five years. His family did not know whether he was alive or dead for three and one-half of these years because he was listed in the records simply as missing in action.

After his release and return home Kavanaugh found himself, along with seven other former POWs, charged with aiding and conspiring with the enemy while being held at a prision camp near Hanoi called the "Plantation." The man who filed the charges against the eight men was the senior POW officer at the camp. The accusation was that Kavanaugh was identified on radio Hanoi in a broadcast on November 11, 1972, as having made a statement urging President Nixon to sign the Paris peace agreement and again on March 5, 1972, as having sent a letter to Vietnam News Service approving anti-war activities.

Although he declined for the most part to talk with reporters after his return to his home town, Kavanaugh did state in a rare interview that he was not guilty and that he had not done any of the things for which he was being accused.

Plagued with the fear about the unknown element in his immediate future and unable to bear the possibility of further imprisonment, the young marine took his own life.

A private physician who examined Sergeant Kavanaugh only an hour before he shot himself reported the young marine to be in perfect physical condition but stated that he had expressed a fear that the military would invent some excuse to hold him in the service. He found this threat to his newly found freedom unbearable. Kavanaugh was the second POW to take his own life during the early months after returning home. He left behind a wife and a young daughter.

It may seem insensitive to speak in abstract generalities about tragic human circumstances. Nevertheless, if we flesh out the skeletal data with a few humane assumptions, certain philosophic issues on death and suicide can be made on the exclusive basis of these newspaper accounts.

What may have precipitated the suicide was Kavanaugh's experience of a growing, perhaps even a complete sense of foundationlessness; perhaps the total and permanent loss of a home, or the discovery that there never had been a home in the first place.

Living in the "Plantation" was likely to have given Abel Kavanaugh an exaggerated sense of the importance of "home," "back home," "the folks back home"; an increased nostalgia for "his country," "his outfit," and so forth. These ideas and images were probably all the emotional support that he had left in prison. As a result, his ground-edness, his sense of foundation and support, consisted, during his imprisonment, of a vastly exaggerated image of how much he actually was loved in his country and supported in his sacrifice by the "folks back home."

Betrayal

Upon his return, it is very likely that his faith in home, friendship, trust, and love was, in his eyes, betrayed abominably. Part of the blame rested on the ambivalent mood of the nation about the Vietnam war. But a major part of the problem could well have resulted from the exaggeration of the idea of home during his imprisonment, when he was homeless. He came back to find that his illusions regarding groundedness were shattered. Without any philosophical preparation, he experienced the shock of sudden and profound alienation. His bitterness and pain were further intensified when he was accused by a superior officer of treason. Now there no longer existed any foundation in Kavanaugh's world; because he had lost even hope. There was no escape from this situation—because he now *was* home. He must have felt something like this: "I am not standing on anything; I am permanently falling into an eternal abyss. Everything I counted on to sustain me has failed me." And that is not life. Suicide merely makes visible what has been real all the time. Suicide was his rational coping with this eternal falling.

It is probable that the seeds of this experience of total groundlessness were in him long before he joined the Marine Corps, even long before he became an adult. This perception of himself as being without base, totally alienated, totally alone, might well have appeared in some of his early feelings about himself. It is even further conceivable that he joined the Marines to compensate for those very beliefs. Here was a place that would teach him to feel strong, real, concrete. There is a tremendous in-group "buddy" feeling in the Marines. Perhaps his unconscious said to him, "Here in the Marines I will really and finally discover my home, my self." The very decision to join the Marines may indicate an uprootedness, dating perhaps from early childhood. The Marines were then his hope for home.

Kavanaugh may have been proud to go through the kind of suffering which basic training provided so that he could prove what a good, strong, solid person he was. Then he came home after proving himself further in the war and found that all of his images of strength and identity and solidarity were false, betrayed. His world view, his most basic patterns of perception, burst like a bubble. And when that happened suicide was for him a logical step. In truth he was nothing. He was but empty space. Life was an illusion, and he wanted to deceive himself no longer. "I am nothing, I do not wish to be a shell. I will therefore make myself truly into nothing."

Existential Counseling

If a therapist or a philosopher had a person like Kavanaugh in treatment or in philosophic counseling, how would he use existential ideas about death to help his patient? First of all, the commitment to therapy is an answer already. Once a person says, "I want you to understand me. I have a problem," he is less likely to be dangerously suicidal. At that moment the patient is searching for another foundation: a relationship. And that is a realistic search and is often the beginning of an answer. A hopelessly suicidal person will not take the crucial healing step of crying, "help!" No one can force a person to take that first step. We can strap him in a straitjacket, but we cannot force him to ask for help. That step is based on his freedom, which is part of his integrity as a human being.

Let us say a person does take that crucial first step and comes to someone for philosophic help—to a counselor, philosopher, psychotherapist, psychiatrist, minister, or friend. How would an existentially and phenomenologically oriented individual respond? First of all, the request for help puts a tremendous burden on anyone. Many a conscientious counselor would feel, perhaps incorrectly, that the patient's life is in his hands. And that is a most difficult position to be in. And Kavanaugh presents a special case. An authentic counselor might feel that the conscience of the country is speaking through him. He would feel that as an American he owes this individual a tremendous debt. It would almost be as if he himself were in a prison camp. Would he be able to tolerate that? Would he have the strength to take on the responsibility of dealing with such a deep-lying and tragic problem?

It would take a near-saint to be such a person's therapist. The therapist, even though he may be competent, might take evasive action, feeling the burdens of undertaking such a difficult therapeutic problem. And this would have its effect on the patient, because he would interpret the therapist's hesitancy as a further rejection.

Nevertheless, with this background, and assuming an existential counselor who has made a commitment to him, the following thoughts about treatment are relevant.

The Treatment

Kavanaugh left behind a wife and a daughter. Undoubtedly his wife was presented with a tremendously difficult and probably unfair responsibility when Kavanaugh came home. In effect, the country said to her, "you take care of your husband for us. No one can really make up for what he has experienced, but you, who waited long and painfully, must now make him whole again." That she could not possibly provide such care is obvious—for Kavanaugh killed himself. But if he had sought philosophic counseling, I believe the key to the type of treatment he received would have been in the existence of his daughter. I would stress that theme as strongly as I could. Most people have strong feelings about children—about the child in them, about their own children, about the children in their society, and about the world's children. This attachment I believe is a universal phenomenon.

What a person does will be witnessed by his or her child; what he does to himself he will teach that child about himself. What he does will be a permanent part of the child's life. He is condemned irrevocably to be the one of the two people most vital in teaching the child how a human being, a parent, copes—or fails to cope—with the unjust stresses of life. Kavanaugh's daughter, I believe, *was* his meaning. *She* depended on him, even though he was not with her all the time. He was part of *her* image of home. *She* was his witness, dependent on him and the extension of his consciousness. She—because she represented a greater amount of hope than he did—might probably have been perceived by Kavanaugh as a greater reality than he.

And when Kavanaugh thought about his daughter to give meaning to his life, he would realize that she depended on him for much of the meaning in her own life. He would think of her as an extension of himself; and it would make no difference if she was pretty or ugly, healthy or ill, normal or crippled, bright or dull. What would have mattered was that he make a father-to-daughter commitment to her. He is irreplaceable to her. There is no way she can have a substitute for him. Any substitute is precisely that—a substitute father.[1]

---

[1] Is "father" a commitment, a symbol, or a biological reality? The facts are clear: A nonbiological father, one who has made a commitment only (as in the case of adoption)

This existential approach—focusing the treatment method on his daughter—might have helped Kavanaugh to put his entire life in a different perspective. It might have given him the ground he did not have in prison and which was then betrayed at home. His daughter's need for a father might have been the foundation on which his meaning and his life could have rested. In this way he might have given meaning not only to his life at present, but also retroactively or retrospectively. It may also have put his prison experience, his joining the Marines, and his lost childhood in a different context. Through his child he might have discovered that in the context of his total life his own childhood was more important than the Marines, and more important even this atrocious prison experience.

What is it that he might have discovered in talking and thinking about his daughter? He would have discovered that what is important and what is real was not he himself, his ego, his joining the Marines, or whatever, but his *consciousness*—and his consciousness would have been evoked in his relationship with his daughter. His consciousness would have been brought most clearly to the surface by the intersubjective, or the intimacy, or the encounter dimension of consciousness. His realization that there was a relationship between him and his daughter, and that this relationship was irreplaceable to both, might have given him meaning and a foundation to his life. Both he and his daughter might have then discovered that they participated in a higher stream of consciousnesss, their common ground and foundation. And that conscious relationship and that participation would have been perceptible to him as more real and more significant than his prison experience, the Marines, or the nation.

We have now covered a multitude of suggestions on how to respond positively to death. And we have come to understand that to experience the strength of individuality is vital. That is why we can say, even at the risk of sentimentality, that our cheery-eyed cancer patient was able to view her death as a going-away party. Now we will have a section in which you will be asked to review the important points in our discussion of finding an answer to death.

---

is not the same as a father who has made a commitment and who at the same time is her biological father. Similarly, part of the world for an adopted child is that her biological father (if he is alive) opted against her. The hard impact of these facts can be softened. We can compensate for these facts; but we cannot erase them. These facts and realities should be emphasized in philosophical counseling.

REMEMBER

1. Death leads to meaning (Chapter 4).
2. Death reveals (Chapter 4):
    a. Your guilt about unfulfilled potential, especially intellectual and artistic development, political and social achievements, and bodily pleasures.
    b. Your needs for identity and individuality.
    c. The importance of intimacy.
    d. The danger of worthlessness and self-hatred.
    e. Your mystical possibilities.
    f. Your need for self-knowledge.
    g. Your permanent need for growth.
    h. Your aloneness.
    i. Your need for a home.
    j. Your need for peace.
3. Death leads us to understand the ethics of detachment (Chapter 5).
4. Death is managed through philosophy rather than pills (Chapter 6).
5. Death unlocks the secrets of consciousness (Chapter 6).
6. Death gives you a task, a destiny, and a purpose in life (Chapter 7).
7. Death teaches you (Chapter 7):
    a. To perceive pain as self-willed.
    b. To come to terms with evil.
8. Death has been perceived as (Chapter 7):
    a. Macabre.
    b. The gentle comforter.
    c. The gay deceiver.
    d. An automaton.
9. Death has been managed by (Chapter 7):
    a. Depression.
    b. Displacement.
    c. Sorrowing.
    d. Being overcome.
    e. Participation.
10. Death can reconstruct the meaning of your past (Chapter 9).
11. Death enables you to have hope for the future (Chapter 9).
12. Death makes possible ego-transcending achievements (Chapter 9).
13. Death can be perceived as an invention (Chapter 10).
14. Death holds you responsible for being yourself (Chapter 10).
15. Death holds you responsible for what troubles you (Chapter 10).

16. Death can be perceived as self-willed (Chapter 10).
17. Death gives us the strength and wisdom to manage the problem of suicide (Chapter 11).
18. Death clarifies the issues of (Chapter 11):
    a. Home.
    b. Encounter.
    c. Responsibility.
    d. Hope.

Exercises

Exercises that will connect you with the experiences of death include the following:

1. Write and analyze your ideal and your realistic obituary (Chapter 4).
2. Examine your reaction to a traumatic or tragic story (Chapter 8).
3. Visualize your funeral (and rebirth) (Chapter 8).
4. Write the script for your own death, including where and how (Chapter 8).
5. Write down the age at which you will die (Chapter 8).
6. Write your autobiography (Chapter 9).

In Part Two we have examined how the anticipation of dying can give meaning to living. We now turn to the other revelation of death: the nature of our eternal inward consciousness. However, before we can fully appreciate the discussion of immortality or deathlessness, we must develop a sense of the awareness or the consciousness that we are. Part Three is devoted to that task.

PART THREE

CONSCIOUSNESS
AND
THE INDIVIDUAL

12

What is Consciousness ?

Before we can embark on an exposition of what an existential-phenomenological philosophy means by consciousness, we must consider the problems of clarity and precision. It is difficult to find the right language for a discussion of consciousness.

THE PROBLEMS WITH CLARITY

It is difficult to be clear and precise in the exposition of the central concept of Part Three of this book, which I here call pure subjective consciousness. Why? Because clarity is a characteristic of the ego, the personality, the world—that is to say, of one of the principal *objects of* consciousness rather than of consciousness itself. In fact, clarity and objectivity lose their meaning when they are applied to the strange, unique, and yet philosophically central activity of *consciousness reflecting upon itself.* This state of affairs may be most unfortunate; be that as it may, the facts of experience with which philosophy concerns itself cannot be changed to suit the limitations of language.

Furthermore, clarity and precision are aspects of what we call the analytic form of thinking, and analytic thinking is based on clear definitions. But what does it mean to define? As the very word indicates, it means to *delimit,* to *make finite.* In other words, to be clear means to exclude, to isolate one item out of a vast array of possibilities and then show with distinctness what this item is *not.* Analytic thinking is useful in dealing with things, with objects, which are isolated entities. However, when we investigate consciousness, which is pervasive and all-encompassing, and which is insurmountably subjective and reflexive, then the conventional process of definition becomes irrelevant; the demand for clear definition, rather than facilitating, obstructs the lucid exposition of the structure of consciousness.

There is another consideration. When we talk about concepts such as the "Eternal Now," "pure consciousness," or "being," we are really talking about everything, are we not? At the very least, we are talking about the matrix, the background, or the space-time in which everything exists and occurs. And when we talk about everything we talk about *being*. Clarity is a characteristic of particulars, rather than of the totality—of individuals, rather than of the universal. Being, like consciousness, is an indefinable term.

In fact, when talking about the totality of *being*, the demand for clarity becomes almost irrelevant. The demands for precision and clarity are based on the pre-existing confusion between consciousness and its objects, because it is that confusion which tells us that the world consists of objects rather than fields. But it is also precisely this confusion that we are trying to clear up. To require clarity and objectivity in the exposition of consciousness makes sense only when the pure subjective consciousness is mistaken for a particularized individual ego—that is, when consciousness, which is not an object but a subject, is artificially made and distorted into an object. And it is this systematic error, this "category mistake," from which a phenomenological philosophy seeks to protect us.

Such is also the point that Plato makes in his famous *Allegory of the Cave*. The prisoner, who sees that what everyone thinks of as real is only shadows on the screen, tries to explain the truth to his friends: the experience of having left the cave and perceived the sun. In order to explain to them that what they saw and thought was real were in fact shadows—and that the reality is the sun, which they had never seen—the prisoner is however forced to use the language of the shadows. He describes consciousness (the sun) by using the language of the *objects* of consciousness (the shadows). That is a task of almost insurmountable difficulty.

In sum, the first step in describing consciousness is to establish the fact that the task cannot really be fulfilled without doing violence to language and to thinking. And this is the problem that we must also face here.

Everything I am going to say about consciousness is essentially meaningless. Such is the origin of what is called negative theology, the activity in which theologians, saints, and holy men engage when they talk in paradoxes and contradictions. Their claim is that everything we can *say* about the mystical experience or, in this case, of the experience of consciousness, is false. I agree. I use such words as Eternal Now, pure consciousness, subjectivity, reflexive thinking, etc. But these words are approximations only. They are metaphors and guidelines, perhaps useful and helpful in this context, but never absolutely accurate and precise. They are misunderstood whenever they are understood.

These considerations may assuage some of the critics of the phenomenological approach to philosophy, in which "reflexive" or "reductive" thinking about "intentional" consciousness is inevitably clothed in the garments of obscure language. (These terms will be defined in the next section.)

A DISTINCTION BETWEEN CONSCIOUSNESS
AND ITS OBJECTS

I would like now to explore the relationship of consciousness to the phenomenon of death in more detail and hope that this will lead us to an understanding of the indestructibility of consciousness, or the "Eternal Now." That may well be one of the most important ways to find an answer to death.

Let me try to evoke a sense of what consciousness is by emphasizing now the distinction between *consciousness* and the *objects of consciousness*. If you ask a philosopher to define existentialism for you he will tell you existentialism is but one application of the method of phenomenology. And if you ask him to define phenomenology for you, he will tell you that in the last analysis phenomenology is but a theory of the nature and the importance of consciousness. And if you ask that philosopher further, What *is* his theory of consciousness, he will tell you that the phenomenological theory of consciousness is the theory of the *intentionality* of consciousness. Then if you ask him, What *is* the intentionality of consciousness—really pinning him down, now—he will answer: All consciousness is consciousness of *something*. That is the theory of the intentionality of consciousness. That is the bedrock on which the existential-phenomenological movement rests. But what does it mean? Why is that statement important? It is here that we must start defining the distinction between consciousness and the objects of consciousness.

The statement that all consciousness is consciousness of something means that all experience consists of two poles: consciousness *and* its objects. First, there can be no consciousness without it "ending in" an object. There can be no awareness without it "landing on" or "leading to" an object. We cannot see light unless the electromagnetic radiation collides with an object. Only when the streams of radiation are reflected from objects are they seen as light. And we saw in Chapter 6 that separation anxiety results when we try to remove an object from the consciousness to which it is "attached." The removal of the object, an act which forces the disclosure of consciousness *per se,* is then also the experience of ultimate anxiety. Thus, no consciousness can really exist without it also "landing" on an object. Nevertheless, the effort we make to think about consciousness rather than of its objects is called reflexive or reductive (stepping-back) thinking. And it is that kind of unconventional, unorthodox, and hard-to-define thinking we must do in order to grasp the meaning of pure consciousness.

Second, and more important for our definition of consciousness as intentionality, is the converse of the above position: there can be no object without a string of consciousness being "attached" to it. *There can exist no thing without that thing at the same time being an object of some consciousness.* This position resembles idealism. Every object has attached to it a stream of consciousness, connecting it with some ego. Unless an object connects to some ego, we cannot meaningfully assert even that the object exists. I call this the comet theory of objects.[1] Every object is like a comet that has a tail, and that tail is the conscious stream that connects it with some subjectivity. In other words, we cannot explain the world in terms of objects alone. We must explain the world by also referring to the existence of a pervasive sea of consciousness. But that consciousness is different from the world. It is not *part* of the world, it is not *in* the world—because it *views* the world, it *sees* the world. It is *not* in the world in the sense in which objects are in the world. William James invented a felicitous phrase for describing consciousness phenomenologically: he called it the "stream of consciousness."

Later, when we discuss alienation, we will find that the theory of the intentionality of consciousness provides a philosophical explanation for that psychological and sociological condition.

DREAMS

Dreams are one of the most beautiful metaphors that we can use to understand the relationship of our individual subjective consciousness to its objects. Why do we dream? It is as if we inject dreams into the

---

[1] *Managing Anxiety* (Englewood Cliffs, N.J.: Prentice-Hall, 1974), Chapter 1.

world to remind us of our true philosophic nature. As we saw in Chapter 10, we create ourselves, in the sense that we choose our finitude. But this act of self-creation involves an act of self-deception, because we also *forget* that we are the creator. Nevertheless, we leave a clue behind: Our dreams are the reminder of our philosophic nature. When we study the mystery of dreaming, we are able to "remember"—in the Platonic sense in which learning is really remembering the Eternal Forms among which our soul lived before incarnate birth—the cosmic, metaphysical, or ontological possibilities of ourselves.

In your dream, which you invent while you are asleep and which is an object and a product of your consciousness, there are many people—*including you*. But the you in the dream is not the real you. In truth, the *stream* of consciousness is you, which is both asleep and dreaming. The *content*, or the objects of that consciousness, is now not the real world but is the people in the dream—including you. It is obvious that all of these people are in one sense "inventions": they all are your creations, your constructions. Dream analysis in therapy can use this approach to help the patient assume responsibility for his dreams. None of these dream figures is "real" as live people are real—that is, in the sense of being an independent *subjective stream* of consciousness in addition to the *objects* which they are to that conscious flow. What is also "invented" by you who are the subjective stream of consciousness is your *identification* with one of those figures as being you. Let us say there are ten people and two animals in your dream. In truth, they all have exactly the same relationship to you. They are all supported in their existence by being objects to your *one* inward and subjective conscious stream. All of them are your "inventions." However, *you select one of them and say, "That's me."* This selection may indeed be done passively; you feel nevertheless responsible for that selection. It defines your personality and your lifestyle and *it can be changed.* The name of that change is growth or success in psychotherapy. The object with which you identify yourself need not be physically similar to the real bodily you; it can resemble someone else. You can even choose one of the animals in your dream to be you. In short, you identify yourself, you confuse yourself with one of the elements in the dream. And once this is done you start *living* the dream rather than *reflecting* on the dream. That is what we mean when we say you are dreaming.

You cannot ask questions—philosophical questions—within the dream, such as "Am I really someone else?" "Am I dreaming?" etc. The "dream you" cannot ask a "dream friend" in your dream, "Are we really the same? Was there a dream before in which I appeared as someone else? Will there be another dream in which I will appear as someone else?" If these questions were indeed asked in the dream, then they would be meaningless because the wrong person is asking them. It is the dream figure who is asking, rather than the you who is asleep—the true subjective consciousness. All of these questions become rather meaningless when the wrong person—the one-dimensional thing, the non-person—is asking them. It is the dream figure that is asking the question when the person who should really be asking is the you who are asleep; the consciousness, and not its objects.

As long as you do not separate the consciousness upholding the dream from the dream figures, you are dreaming. You are dreaming as long as you identify your consciousness with one of the dream figures. To wake up is to realize that the dream figures are different from the dreaming consciousness. Similarly, using the metaphor of a higher-level spiritual alarm clock, we can say that the person who is in touch with his pure consciousness has awakened from the dream of his everyday identification with his body, his feelings, and with the other worldly objects, as well as values and goals.

Let us now examine the belief in reincarnation—which is another significant parable—in terms of this dream metaphor. To believe literally in reincarnation may be the result of a confusion. Using the analogy of the dream, it means that you confuse your *subjective*, conscious self with the changing *content* or object of a series of dreams or with a sequence within one dream. For example, in one dream, you—the universal supporting consciousness—identify yourself with a bear. In a subsequent dream, or in a later episode of the same dream, you identify yourself with a woman. And in a third dream, you are a young boy. Bear, woman, and boy are but some of the *many* objects in the dreams of your *one* subjective consciousness. There is no special connection between the bear, the woman, and the boy which is not also true of relations among the other objects of these dreams. In a sense, all your dream objects are you in that they are "attached" to the object end of your conscious stream *while you exist in a state of self-deception or forgetfulness about the true nature of your consciousness.* The woman in your dream—that is, the object of your consciousness that is the woman—does not remember being a bear! Nor does the boy remember being a woman. Yet, in truth—if the truth is your consciousness—you have in this dream sequence actually experienced reincarnation. But the connection is not "bear-woman-child" but "bear-you, woman-you and child-you." It is the common relation of a plurality of objects to a single subject that provides continuity. Consequently, reincarnation makes sense only if that theory or myth puts you in touch with the Eternal Now; that is, with the objectless consciousness that you are. It is indeed poetic to conceptualize dreams as clues to a transcendental reality (i.e., pure consciousness) which have been scattered by us into the world of objects to remind us of our eternal philosophic essence.

ALIENATION

Let us now return to the subject of alienation. We are strangers in this world. We are alienated from the world. Why? Because in accordance with one important aspect of our essence we do not belong in this world. We are a consciousness as well as a body, and consciousness is not a part of the world of nature. Consciousness is the witness of the world of nature, it is not the world of nature itself. Man, like God, is a transcendental being, not an immanent being. God is transcendental—outside this world. And so is a person, with his consciousness, outside this world. This kind of alienation is natural and healthy, not sick and neurotic. We have here an inevitable alienation which is, in the language of existential phenomenology, ontological rather than pathological.

There was a movie made in 1973 called *The Scarecrow;* it was about two hoboes in search of meaning. This film—as is true of many—can be understood in existential terms. Hoboes, like the rest of us, do not belong. They are aliens in this world, trying to make contact and to create a meaning for themselves. Similarly, to the extent that I am a pure subjective consciousness, I am a stranger in this world. I am not an object in nature. So when I look for answers to the question "Who am I?" in medicine, psychology, anthropology, sociology, and economics, then in fact I search for my true nature only among the objects of this world. But my real nature is to be also *outside* this world. I should therefore consult "outside" experts, "transcendental" and not "empirical" experts, experts in "consciousness" and not in "things" or "objects," if I wish a true answer. As a result of the fact that I am a consciousness, which is free, and not a thing, which is fixed, I am condemned to invent my nature. Because freedom can never become a thing, that project is ultimately bound to fail—as it also happened in the film. The movie begins with a hobo carrying a gift package—a lamp. Six years ago this man made a girl pregnant and then left her;

now, after six years, he wants to see his child. He does not even know if it is a boy or a girl. The film is the story of his pilgrimage. When he finally finds her there is an emotional scene in which the girl curses him and tells him, falsely, that she is married.

Then the ultimate revenge is hers. He is a devout Catholic and he asks about the child, "Is it a boy or a girl?" She responds with a cruel lie. She says that the child died in childbirth, that it was a boy, and that he was never baptized. While she tells him this lie their son is playing peacefully next to the telephone in his mother's apartment, unaware of the devastating emotional catastrophe occurring beside him. These bitter and tragic words demolish the father and he leaves. The woman was expressing her anger; perhaps she would have relented in a while; but he will never know the truth. There is no way she can ever find him again.

There follows a violent scene in which the hobo grabs a young boy and tries to baptize him in a fountain; then he goes berserk and finally falls into a coma. His meaning has not been fulfilled. The lamp is never delivered. He is an alien, a stranger in search of meaning, and his only meaning was to have come from giving the gift to his child, and to find out whether it was a boy or girl. He has been totally frustrated in his search for meaning. And yet the situation was fully his responsibility, because he chose to leave the girl he had made pregnant.

This pattern is a prototype of the existential view of the human condition. To be human is to be alienated, a condition that we now see follows inevitably from the very structure of the field of consciousness itself. We can thus understand the alienation of consciousness from the world; consciousness is intrinsically different from the world. We can also understand the alienation from meaning, since meaning is self-given, self-assigned, and therefore always doubtful: we need absolute and final answers, but we do not have them. A human being is indeed, by nature, an alien, as Camus expressed in his book *The Stranger* and Antonioni in his film *The Passenger*. He will always be frustrated in his attempt to finally reach and identify with the world and with meanings. He will be as frustrated as our hobo was frustrated in reaching his child.

Let us not forget that the structure of the field of consciousness, while explaining man's alienation from the world, also explains how reunion or homecoming—the integration of pure consciousness with its world—can be achieved. We will talk about this now.

THE CONTINUITY OF CONSCIOUSNESS AND THE WORLD

There is another side in the relationship of consciousness to its objects. Consiousness is also *continuous* with and *connected* to the world. There is always paradox. Consciousness is like a tree, with its roots in the soil—the world. Consciousness is intertwined with the world. There can be no consciousness without an object, so that if you experience your connectedness with the world, then you will not feel that you are a stranger to this world, but you will feel that you are part of the ecosystem, that you *belong* here. Then the ideas of leading a thoroughly involved life, of having goals of participation, make sense.

But the hobo is the alienated individual. To abandon a pregnant woman is unrealistic—that is, irresponsible. It means he is not in touch with the world outside his consciousness. Also, to build an entire life around the goal of getting back to her six years later is equally unrealistic, almost schizoid. His consciousness is withdrawn from the world; it does not participate in the world. The hobo—the scarecrow—was just a shadow of a man, a straw man, and not in touch with what is real in the world and outside his consciousness. He is out of touch on two counts: he does not achieve his goal—his contact with social reality and value structures—which is to see his child. Also, his general approach to the conduct of life and to relationships with others lacks the sense of responsibility that is the hallmark of recognizing their hard and independent reality. He is removed from the world in the sense that his consciousness seems to be out of touch with its objects; it is dislocated from its expected intertwined involvement and connectedness with objects. If we are in touch with what is real—that is, if we emphasize the *connectedness* of consciousness, then a life of realistic involvement in the world is possible.

However, the main topic of this chapter is the consciousness that is *not* in touch with the world; the one that has been separated, severed from the world, alienated, without being schizophrenic. Alienation, when total and uncontrollable, is an illness. It does serve, however, to illuminate the meaning of pure consciousness. I have tried to evoke that alienation as an experience in you, one which illuminates the answer to death that is called immortality. The distinction between consciousness and the objects of consciousness, if properly understood, can give us further insight into the eternal and indestructible character of the pure inward and subjective consciousness aspect of that continuity. That is the issue of immortality, which will be discussed in due time.

13

Consciousness
and the World

WHERE IS CONSCIOUSNESS?

Another approach to the elucidation of pure consciousness is to explore some of its relations to the world and to examine how it interpenetrates the objects in the world. We can facilitate the experiential and conceptual exposition of pure consciousness by asking the heuristic questions, *Where* is the transcendental ego? Where is awareness or consciousness?[1] These are "catalytic" questions, whose purpose it is to elicit in us experientially the disclosure of consciousness. As is the case with a catalyst, mulling over the question precipitates the experience of an answer. The Zen masters used this type of question, called the Koan (e.g. "What is the sound of one hand clapping?"), which always had a nonsensical answer, "*wu*." The implication is that the question should not be raised or that a wholly new world with entirely new possibilities opens up. The question, where is my consciousness? functions as that kind of an exercise; it can help us to understand and experience the structure of consciousness.

Sartre refers to consciousness as "nonpositional." With respect to the world, even the universe, consciousness does not have a "place." We cannot draw its coordinates. We cannot map the universe and then say, "In a map of the universe consciousness resides *right here*." Consciousness is real, and it is you—but it is not in and of the world. Consciousness is not the world and its objects, but it is *the seeing of the*

[1] The term "transcendental ego" is the phenomenological-existential term for the pure consciousness that is at the center of my ego. The transcendental ego is the consciousness that is a "pure look" and can never be an object.

world. These are basic facts of human experience, facts with vast consequences.

We might compare the idea of a nonpositional consciousness to a completely circular (360) screen. We are literally surrounded by film and screen and we ask, "Where is the projector?" Well, the projector is not "in" or "on" the screen. The film covers the entire world, as it were, and the camera is nowhere to be found on the screen. The projector is *outside* the world of the screen. In parallel fashion, even if our awareness covers the whole universe, the transcendental ego, while completely real, is nevertheless not *in* the universe. There exists no *place* which is the position of consciousness. The consciousness that is the observer of the universe is strictly nonpositional, where "position" refers to a coordinate point in the world so observed.

If we now ask the question, Where is consciousness? with respect to human beings (that is, we expect to find it somewhere in the body), then a presuppositionless description of subjective experience answers that consciousness is pre-human, post-human, or trans-human. What does that mean? Our question about the location of consciousness has now been transformed into a question about its place in the human body or in the person. Consciousness, with respect to the body and the person (what in existential phenomenology we call the empirical or psychological ego), is also nonpositional. The implication of this descriptive insight is also of the greatest significance, because it asserts that "I" am "nowhere."

Consciousness as Pre-Human

Consciousness, in and by itself, is not human. Humanness and personality are "invented" with the postulation of birth and death. I call that phenomenon an archetypal decision. Personhood is created through limitation. Consciousness remains forever ambivalent. It recognizes and experiences its other-worldly or nonworldly transcendental character; but it also perceives itself as a concrete human existence thrown into a particular situation. In the words of Heidegger, humanness is a being-there *(Dasein)* whose existential nature it is to be thrown into a world *(in-der-Welt-sein)*. Only through the acceptance of limits does our humanity emerge. The ego is constructed through negation. Personality results from self-forgetful identification with a concrete area of the world of objects, delimited by specific spatiotemporal conceptions of a birth and a death. This position will be explained later.

In the last analysis, consciousness is beyond that which is human; it transcends the human. Consciousness is pre-human in that it is consciousness itself that is responsible for creating the sense of humanity. It is post-human in that consciousness is also de-organized, de-constituted, and disembodied humanity. That is to say, consciousness appears after (post) philosophical analysis of our limited humanness; and it is trans-human in that consciousness can go beyond our humanity into distant history and into infinite space and time.

If we now ask the question, Is existentialism a humanism?[2] (asked by Sartre and answered by Heidegger) my answer is both "yes" and "no." Existentialism is exclusively a humanism only to the historian who wants to give it a label and argue that because existentialism discusses the human condition it must be a humanism. I call that view conventional, atheistic, or individualistic existentialism. But a deeper look tells us that existentialism is a pre-, post-, and trans-humanism. It is here that existentialism shows its dependence on transcendental phenomenology and shows traces of idealism. That deeper searching also tells us that our essence as persons is not only to be human beings and thus members of the order of nature, but it is also to be consciousness—and consciousness is not necessarily human. Consciousness is the observer of the universe that *can* confuse or identify itself with an individual person but *need not* make such a commitment or cathexis. Consciousness is that mysterious power that can limit itself and identify itself and forget itself (or deceive itself) in such a way that it creates the sense of existing as an individual human being in the world. (The technical terms for these possibilities of consciousness are, respectively, *finitude, cathexis,* and *self-deception.*)

Blood Vessels

To continue this elucidation of the important phenomenon of consciousness I shall draw another metaphor. Let me call it a metaphor for cosmic consciousness. Imagine a long, thick, heavy horizontal line which, in its "human" region, has a three-dimensional bulge; cosmic consciousness is like a thick nerve which at the point of becoming human spreads itself out into many smaller nerves and then regroups them together again into one thick strand. Or, cosmic consciousness is like an artery which, when it reaches the "decision to be human," divides itself into many capillaries, which then converge again into a sin-

---

[2] Humanism is a modern, nontheistic, rationalist movement that holds that man is capable of self-fulfillment, ethical conduct, etc., without recourse to supernaturalism.

gle vein. These images are meant to suggest the eternal stream of consciousness, which is the history and evolution of space-time. It is symbolized by the thick nerve or the blood in the artery that, upon becoming an historical and situational event, splits itself into innumerable individual streams. Each of those individual capillaries—beginning with the arteries and ending in the veins—is like an individual finite and alienated life, a person (see diagram).

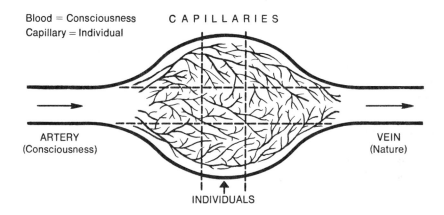

The following anecdote must be received as an aesthetic experience with a philosophic message: One day, while I was walking to my office, I felt suddenly and inexplicably that the burden and weight of living had been lifted. I felt supported. The burden of living was no longer mine alone. In fact, I had ceased to be a conventional existentialist, in that I gave up the excesses of individualism associated with that position. I sensed a current stronger than me and one in which I *participated*, a current within me of which I am only a part and which supports me as the sea supports a ship. I became a transcendental, or a religious existentialist, a kind of mystical phenomenologist. At that brief moment it became intuitively clear to me that the religious positions that there is a God, that I can participate in His life, and that I am not really different from God but a part of Him, made sense. I felt that as my body was supported by nature, so my individual awareness was supported by a cosmic consciousness.

Also, at that moment it was no longer necessary for me to be self-reliant and independent. The burdens of being the source of my own definition, of choosing and defining myself, of creating my own essence, of withstanding cosmic loneliness were all lifted. Why? Because I was not the capillary alone, which had to define what is meant to be a capillary, but somehow I was an integral part of the total blood-stream. At that moment I felt connected with all reality, physical and spiritual, and the burden, aloneness, and cynicism associated with conventional existentialism—the philosophy of freedom, individuality, and self-reliance—vanished. Did I at that moment lose my freedom? No, but I did lose the sense that I was a capillary cut off from the universal bloodstream. I had a sense of continuity with all of Being, rather than the sense of separateness and alienation.

This sense of oneness emerges if we go beyond the human or personal to the transpersonal; it appears if we are open to the transcendental dimension (that is, the subjective zone of pure consciousness) of experience. This sense of oneness can be recognized as a real therapeutic possibility only because pure consciousness becomes for existentialism a genuine category of explanation.

Aloneness and Unity

In my opinion, the philosophy of conventional existentialism—a philosophy of alienation and individuality, emphasizing man's aloneness—and the philosophies of transcendental phenomenology and mysticism—holding that man is one with all of Being and that Being supports and cares for him—are both deep and valid insights. These views are represented by Sartre and Marcel, respectively. The former views human existence through the eyes of atheism, alienation, and self-reliance, whereas the latter perceives human life through the eyes of theism, communion, and participation. These views represent disparate, but equally necessary and real poles of being; both world views add up to one dialectic of Being. Both poles are real and they co-exist in the vast range of consciousness, in the dance of man and God. I see no reason why these two views cannot be seen as extensions of one another and as complements to one another. Both have their measure of truth. Both must be integrated into one total, synthesized world view. They are reminiscent of what Niels Bohr defined as his Principle of Complementarity or Correspondence.[3]

The difference between the conventional existential and the transcendental oriental view is a dialectical oscillation between individual consciousness and cosmic consciousness. The supreme meditation exercise would then be one that helps you to oscillate between individual consciousness—elicited by a "Who-am-I" exercise—and cosmic consci-

---

[3] This principle asserts that quantum mechanics and Newtonian physics are two ways of expressing the same physical reality as long as we deal with everday objects.

ousness—elicited by the immortality exercises that will be found at the end of this book.

PURE CONSCIOUSNESS

Consciousness, in its purity can best be experienced when the body is relaxed.

Relaxation Exercises

The more relaxed your body, the more ready you will be to experience and reflect on the pure inward and subjective consciousness that you are. You can induce deep relaxation through anything that *distracts* your awareness from the fact that you are identified with a body. Specifically, the following suggestions and exercises will decrease your consciousness of your body by making it feel more similar to its environment than is usual.

You can achieve deep relaxation through the suggestion that you are very, very heavy. Imagine that you are resting very comfortably and that you are very heavy, that gravity is really tying you down, and that this sense of heaviness eliminates your desire to be active and neutralizes your sense of differentiation from your environment. Imagine that an infinite number of ropes are pulling you down, and every cell is pulled down; you feel the gravity in every cell of your body. And as you are experiencing yourself in that way, your body becomes almost secondary—you feel almost outside your body, because your body has now become immobilized and you have lost all commitment to be active. You are like Gulliver, who awakes only to find himself tied down by the Lilliputians. You have now given up thinking of yourself as a mobile body. You leave your body behind and thus you become a disembodied consciousness.

Another way to suggest deep relaxation to yourself is to influence your cardiovascular system to feel great bodily warmth, heat. You are afire. You are feverish. You are *hot.* You may literally feel an unusual tingling in many of your organs. And when you feel that hot tingling, you again move to being the observer of your body. You then do not identify with your body, but you experience yourself perhaps as hovering above it, or on its surface—you leave your body behind.

These are *deep* relaxation exercises. Success depends on experience. You may start to twitch, to feel uncomfortable, because you are accustomed to perceive your body as an instrument of locomotion, or an instrument for escape—but not as something to be temporarily abandoned.

Another way of achieving a sense of deep relaxation is to think of yourself as a rag doll: go through each organ, each muscle and limb of your body, and let them become completely limp. Imagine that all of you is like a rag doll. Begin with your neck and continue with the muscles surrounding your ears, then your ears, and your scalp muscles, etc. Gradually descend in this fashion all the way down to your toes. Again you will have abandoned a sense of identification with your body. Your subjective conscious center will feel that it has detached itself from the now almost unreal body. You can perform these exercises one after the other. They are difficult; to get the maximum benefit from them requires much training—but you can learn how to do them.

Another way of achieving the experience of the pure subjective consciousness that you are is to close your eyes and then put something over them. This has the effect of turning your gaze inward, suggesting that your consciousness is turned inward. Then you are ready for the exploration of inner space. At this moment consciousness begins to become visible by itself, detached. And you must continue the exercise by focusing on your breathing.

The Philosophical Importance of Breathing

Philosophically, breathing is one of our most interesting activities. Breathing helps us to move away from our identification with the world and thus puts us in touch with our conscious centers. Breath is the essence of human life; therefore, detachment from breath, which occurs when we observe it, leads us into the experience of isolated consciousness in its purity.

Breath means life. There is perhaps no death more horrible than suffocation. Life is breathing. If you stop breathing just long enough to feel uncomfortable, then you will quickly move to terror. Breathing is almost coeval with existence; it is almost the experience of Being itself.

Moreover, breathing is almost spiritual—though in fact it is a material phenomenon—because it involves something we cannot see. If there is any material substance in this world which comes close to being spirit or consciousness, it is air. Some cultures do not even have words for air, it is so much taken for granted—like space, or consciousness itself. If we want to develop a philosophical position which holds that consciousness is not something that exists deeply and mysteriously inside our bodies, but that it is continuous with the world, then what better metaphor can we think of than air? Air is the "spirit" that is both outside *and* inside. Breathing is the one obvious area in which the outer and the inner worlds are in touch, where the inner and outer boundaries overlap, where what is outside and what is inside are interchanged. If we are in the same room, then what was in your lungs is now in my lungs, and vice versa. What greater sign of intimacy and connectedness is there than to know that we breathe the same air? Thus are we all physically connected.

The act of breathing in and breathing out is thus an excellent physiological metaphor for the intentional subject-object field of consciousness that we are. And detachment from it, which occurs when we *observe* it rather than when we *are* it, is a splendid way of experiencing the Eternal Now that is the essence of our subjective inward consciousness.

Furthermore, my breathing is my speaking; our speaking is made of the air that we share. Many of the important characteristics of consciousness—the pure consciousness that we all are—are revealed to us through a proper understanding of air and breathing. There is more.

Breathing is one of the few phenomena or behavioral patterns of the body that involves both the sympathetic and the autonomic nervous systems. We can, if we wish, control our breathing. Under normal circumstances, we cannot voluntarily control our digestive processes. Nor can we control our heartbeats. But we do control our breathing. Breathing can of course also be automatic, as it is in sleep; thus it becomes an important inducer of hypnotic sleep. Breathing connects the two nervous systems. Breathing exercises, as they are practiced in yoga, for example, are central to achieving a hypnotic state, in which control moves from one nervous system to the other. This transition of nerve impulses from the sympathetic to the autonomic nervous systems can be achieved through breath control, because breathing can be controlled by either system.

There are many ways to achieve control over breathing. One way is to breathe in very deeply. Another is to breathe shallowly, or fast, or slowly, breathing through your nose, your mouth, or breathing slowly in through one nostril and out through the other, as is done in yoga. All kinds of variations are possible. These exercises teach you that you can learn to have control over your breathing. Control over breathing means recognizing that breathing uses the diaphragm (singers know about that), a muscle at the base of the lungs which when we inhale goes down and pushes out the stomach. Learning how to breathe fully is an important experience in achieving deep relaxation.

As you learn to control your breathing, you will experience an immediate reaction. Some people will get dizzy and others will develop a tingling sensation in their extremities, because the oxygen content in the blood is changed.

The Conscious Center

Let us now return to the exposition of pure inward consciousness and how we can experience it through breathing.

Once you have achieved control over your breathing, the essence of your existence, you can go one step further—you can look *at* your breathing. You no longer *are* your breathing, but you now *observe* your breathing. This process is both difficult and powerful, because in observing your breathing you become even "thinner" than your breath and thus you may come the closest that you ever will to being in touch with your pure conscious center, which can also be called the Eternal Now. Now your consciousness observes that which is closest to consciousness—your breathing. At that moment you are in touch with the inmost subjective reality that is your ego, not with any *content* or *object* of consciousness, but with your pure consciousness directly, your transcendental ego.

It follows that observing, controlling, looking at, and reflecting on your breathing and then, as a result, experiencing the pure and detached consciousness that you are, *gives you the other* (the mystical) *answer to death.*[4] You now are in touch with the ultimate observer of existence that you truly are. You are now experiencing yourself as the Eternal Now. You now have the sense of immortality.

The purpose of these reflections on air and breath—found also in hypnosis, yoga, and meditation—is to help you transcend your ordinary ways of interpreting reality and be in touch with your own inward, ultimate reality directly. *Reflecting* on breathing helps you to break through the stained-glass windows that separate you from your inner truth. *Reflection* rather than *being* helps you to be in touch with pure consciousness directly.

And while one reality with which you are now in touch may be the world, other people, your body—the contents or objects of your con-

---

[4] The first being the creation of yourself as a living and committed individual.

sciousness—you are above all now also in touch with your pure inward consciousness itself. And that consciousness is beyond death.

Additional help in understanding pure consciousness can be gained by examining the relationship of consciousness to the brain, since the two are often confused.

14

Consciousness
and the Brain

THE IDEA OF THE BRAIN

Let me attempt a clarification of the phenomenological theory of consciousness with a discussion of the brain. Consider the following quotation. It represents the world view of our culture and it is reflected in our basic assumptions underlying the scientific study of man.

> The brain is the master control, the guiding force behind all of man's actions. It is the seat of all human thought and consciousness. . . . Everything that man has ever been, everything he will be, is the product of his brain. . . . It is the brain that makes man man.
>
> But it took man centuries to comprehend that there was a miraculous mechanism inside his head and begin to investigate its workings. . . .
>
> Man has split the atom, cracked the genetic code and, in a Promethean step unimaginable less than a quarter-century ago, leaped from his own terrestrial home to the moon. But he has yet to solve the mysteries of memory, learning and consciousness or managed to understand himself.
>
> The brain is the newest and perhaps last frontier in man's exploration of himself. Crossing that frontier could have the same impact on humanity as the discovery that the earth was round. . . .
>
> The brain now represents science's greatest challenge. . . . The work of the neuroscientists has already produced an exponential increase in man's understanding of the brain. . . .
>
> Even these accomplishments could seem insignificant once the modern Magellans attain their goal of understanding the brain's functions in thought, memory and in consciousness—the sense of identity that distinguishes man from all other known forms of life. Finding the key to these mysteries of the brain, a discovery that would suddenly explain these functions, . . . might even help man . . . respect himself more than he now does.[1]

[1] Excerpts from "Exploring the Frontiers of the Mind," *Time*, January 14, 1974, p. 50. Reprinted by permission from TIME, The Weekly Newsmagazine; Copyright Time Inc.

The frontier *has* been crossed. In fact, it was crossed even before science became a method of asking questions. Before civilization developed the belief that human beings are bodies—or organisms, or computers, or machines—we knew that we are fields of consciousness primarily. The much-derided anthropomorphisms of primitive man are in truth expressions of the insight that consciousness exists either *prior* to physical objects or at least different from and independent of physical objects.

The breakthrough hoped for by scientists can never come because consciousness can never be understood as a function of material objects. The latter are always one pole of a bipolar field, where the other pole is a unique and qualitatively different subjective consciousness.

CONSEQUENCES

Neither understood nor developed are the consequences for research in human beings that follow from the recognition that we are fields of consciousness. Changes will occur in theories of psychoses and neuroses, of the origins of violence and self-destruction, as well as of schizophrenia, depression, and pain. In these areas brain research already has led to influential discoveries. A new theory of the brain-consciousness relationship will make a genuine contribution.

The systematic errors in the premises of the above quotation can be seen if we make the effort, which is equivalent to the most esoteric and convoluted mental acrobatics, to understand ourselves—to understand the existing person that I am at this moment—in terms of these physiological categories. I cannot understand my sense of subjective identity by thinking only of my brain.

I think of my brain: "three-and-a-half pounds of pinkish-grey material with the consistency of oatmeal." I get ill, nervous, anxious at the thought. Why? I force myself into a foreign, false, contrary-to-fact and inauthentic conceptual system. The anxiety is the pain involved in this impossible and serious form of self-denial, of the rejection of my subjective nature.

Also, my nausea or anxiety is a response to the loss of self. I lose my sense of security and stability. Like a variable in the solution of two equations with two variables, I—the real experiencing self—drop out, disappear. I become totally dependent for my being on the incomprehensible, incredibly complex, and frightfully fragile neurons, glia, chemical reactions, and electric currents in my nervous system.

"Some of the brain's chemical reactions take as little as one-millionth of a second. As many as 100,000 neurons may be involved in transmitting the information that results in as simple an action as stepping back to avoid being struck by an oncoming car. The entire process occurs in less than a second."[2]

To think that what I am, my values, my accomplishments, and the world for which I live depend entirely on such distant, uncontrollable, and delicate operations is the effective total destruction of my sense of being an individual consciousness. There is something deeply counterfactual—that is, untrue to the actual given facts in human experience—in this philosophical view of man.

Finally, the concept that I am a brain is insufficiently analyzed. The total situation is not alone that *I am a brain* but that *I am a consciousness of a brain*. All objects are *given to us* as objects *of consciousness*. Research and theories, photographs, measurements, and observations—all of these data are always objects *to some consciousness*. And that subjective consciousness is as necessary for the existence of the total situation as are the objective data about the brain. Only when these insights, based on the careful description and analysis of human experience—on which all theories of man must ultimately be based—have been fully recognized, accepted, and integrated into our medical and physiological researches and theories, can we arrive at an accurate picture of human existence.

If we wish to understand the truth about human nature we must learn to take the facts of subjectivity and of consciousness seriously. Not only does our culture stress the exclusive reality of our bodies and fail to perceive the value of subjectivity and consciousness, it has no clear understanding whatsoever of what are the universal aspects of everyone's experience to which the words "subjectivity" and "consciousness" correspond. If we say that my subjective consciousness is a feeling, a dream, or an image, we are once more confusing an object of subjective consciousness with the so-called transcendental phenomenon of subjective consciousness itself. We commit the same error of misplaced subjectivity that is manifested when, as in the theories of the brain, we confuse the experience of the reality of our subjective consciousness with theories and images of ourselves. A clear understanding of the subjective consciousness that I am or that flows through whatever it is I call "me" will answer for each of us many of the eternal philosophic questions. For one, it clarifies the meaning of death and answers the question of immortality.

[2] Ibid., p. 55.

ACTIVE VERSUS PASSIVE CONSCIOUSNESS

One further point is in order. To understand the above point is also to understand consciousness. And an understanding of consciousness is necessary to find an answer to death. We must distinguish the active and the passive modes of consciousness. Active consciousness has made the decision, as it were, to identify with the bodily—to be embodied—to cast its fate with the fate of the body. The active consciousness is a participant agent in the world. It requires energy, health, strength, etc. Medical manipulation is essential to this commitment. That is to say, the active consciousness, which has "cathected" the body, requires adequate diet, rest, routine, medical treatments, etc. The fact that it is the active (cathected, engaged, committed, embodied, identified, "thrown"—in the language of Heidegger) consciousness that writes books about the pure or passive consciousness creates many of the logical puzzles and problems of expression and communication that are characteristic of this subject matter.

The passive consciousness, however, never disappears. It remains in sleep, in trance, in illness, and in dying. We can now see the philosophical (as well as practical) importance of meditation exercises. Meditation is the attempt to experience the pure, passive, observer, spectator, detached, disengaged, and disembodied consciousness directly. That is one source of our identity, security, meaning, and value.

Let us now explore in some detail the implications of these insights for our understanding of what it means to be an existing individual in a particular and unique space-time situation. That is the central concern of an orthodox or conventional existentialism.

A MYTH OF CREATION

I shall, in a metaphoric way, describe the relation between consciousness and our personal human existence as it follows from the position developed in this book. This point has also direct applications to understanding immortality, a concept to be discussed in Part Four.

The "truth" about Being is an eternal consciousness in which motion, creation, objectivity, and change make no sense. Eternal consciousness "invents" stories and myths about birth and death (more on this in the next chapter) and creates the concept of a self. It creates an image, a construct, an entity called the ego. It also creates time. And the last step in the creation of what we call man is the confused identification between that consciousness, that Eternal Now, and the temporal entity, the object, the construct that is the ego. Thus, the last step in consciousness' creation of human existence is the construction of forgetfulness, of self-deception or, in the language of psychology, of the unconscious. Both that confusion and the identification are final, and in fact to such an extent that we are now in a state of permanent self-estrangement. At that moment of total self-deception, man is born. And at that moment the project of being human and enjoying it or crying about it arises. The act of deceiving ourselves about the actual relationship between consciousness and its objects is also the act that establishes our individuality, uniqueness, reality, and ultimacy as specific human beings.

And that myth is, I would say, the oldest and the newest, the most important and the most obscure idea in the history of mankind. And it is an idea well worth intense reflection.

Let us approach the issue of the relationship between consciousness and the ego, or the issue of the creation of man, from the point of view of the *empirical ego*, or the "personality." The "empirical ego" is the object-ego. It must be distinguished from the consciousness that perceives this ego without *being* it. This latter subjectivity is called "transcendental ego."

THE CONSTITUTION OF PERSONALITY

The Empirical Ego

My personality, or empirical ego, is made up of my moods, feelings, self-concepts, and hopes, in addition to my body. My empirical ego is hopeful or depressed, getting someplace or no place, satisfied or dissatisfied. My moods are not the pure subjective stream of my consciousness, but are part of the content of consciousness. That content is an object that is called the ego, or, in existential phenomenology, the empirical ego. Feelings are also part of the ego; they are related to moods, but are more specific.

Another very important *object* of my consciousness—in the sense that it can be perceived by consciousness—is my self-concept, or self-image. That self-concept is part of the ego (the empirical ego), and not part of pure consciousness (the transcendental ego). For example, each of us has a very important and potent, but not wholly conscious or clear idea of who he is. We can elicit what that idea is by projective techniques. We also can discover the self-concept operating in a person by observing his behavior. Our self-image is an important part, operationally, of the object of consciousness which we call the ego. Our hopes, attitudes, expectations, anxieties, backgrounds, future, social consciousness, traditions, religious views, memories of mother and father, relationships to siblings—all these aspects of the personality make up the empirical ego. It is extraordinarily important to realize that this ego is a *content* of consciousness, an *object* of the consciousness; it is *not* the stream of consciousness itself, nor is it the source of that stream. The empirical ego is precisely that part of the content of consciousness which, in the decision for being a human existence, is confused with the subjective source of the stream of consciousness (the transcendental ego). We are now ready to expand the insights developed in Chapter 10.

Birth and Death

The essential generating determination of that human existence is tied to learning the concepts of birth and death, specifically my birth and my death. It is therefore extremely instructive to trace back in your own experience how *you* learned about *your* birth, and about how *you* learned about *your* death. Remember, you have never experienced *your birth* or *your death;* I have never experienced my birth or my death. And as usually conceptualized, these two limiting situations which fence off what we call our real existential human situation are also *inexperienceable!*

Think back, if you can, to the time when you first organized your total experience around the concept of your birth. It was at that time also that you organized your total experience around the concept of your death. At that moment the concept that *you* are an ego (an empirical ego)—that you are isolated from your surroundings—was created. It is at that moment that you began to invent the fact that you are an ego. And you developed the self-deception that the empirical or psychological ego that you are is identical with the universal and the eternal consciousness that you also are. In truth, however, the subjective stream of consciousness that you are is quite different from the objective ego that you think you are. Pure consciousness can best be described in terms such as eternity, infinity, or in terms that are associated with God, not in terms of bodies and individual existents.

Psychological Problems

We have here reached a very crucial point, one that contains many of the answers to the problems of human existence. What we call problems of human existence are actually the outgrowth of the confusion between subject and object. Our psychological problems are based on the existence of the empirical ego, an idea that is learned, created, carved out of Being, not indigenous to it. Our psychological problems are due to the concepts of birth and death, which are learned or invented; therefore we cannot solve these problems in terms of the psychological or empirical ego alone. In psychology, the solution is really the problem. We must solve our psychological problems by realizing that they are created in and by the invention of the ego. They develop concurrently with the development of the ego. To use the language of existential phenomenology, our psychological problems are constituted right along with the constitution of the ego.

Our consciousness has the ability to organize the data of experience into things and processes. That is the phenomenological notion of constitution. It also can invent identity or self-definition—which means cathexis or commitment through self-deception. The most important application of constitution is our creation of the images of man. The study of the humanities—history, literature, comparative cultures, religions, and the like—is a sampling of self-concepts, of the images of man from among which significant choices have been and are being made. Pure consciousness, one of whose defining characteristics is to be a freedom, can choose identification, limitation, or cathexis with respect to any of the models of human existence presented to the mind of a belletristically educated person. Hence the importance of the humanities in a respectable education.

These, of course, are mere words. I suggest that it is a sacred task to both understand and experience this point. We are here confronted with an aspect of the perennial philosophy that re-emerges in existentialism and phenomenology. An ancient notion, like an undying archetype, is surfacing once more in contemporary philosophy. This idea has a life of its own. Now and then, in the history of philosophy, it is propelled upward and becomes visible. And we live today in one of those periods when it emerges again, bobbing up to the surface of the waters of history. The living of this idea, the understanding of this concept, the full, clear perception of this reality may well make all else pale in comparison. That idea can answer the problem of death.

Further clarification of pure subjective consciousness and its answer to death can be achieved by examining the relationship between consciousness and the phenomenon of time.

15

Consciousness and Time

TIME

A further theme that I wish to introduce is *time*. The experience of lived time may be an even closer experiential equivalent to our human nature than breathing. While we can argue that pure consciousness is like lived time, we can also maintain that the *observation* of time—that is, our detachment from even time itself—is the experience of an even deeper level of our inward subjective consciousness: namely, the Eternal Now.

To the existentialist, time is an experience and not an abstraction exclusively. If you wish to describe how it feels to be alive, to evoke, perhaps in poetic similes, the experience of living—if you were to describe to a non-human creature how it feels simply to exist—then one of the most basic answers will have to include something about the sense of time. Living, existing, and experiencing my consciousness are really experiences of the passage of time. Lived time is an inner conscious flow that is indescribable, irreducible, untranslatable, ineffable, yet clearly experienceable. Thus, I *am* the passage of time. Time is the most archaic form of the experience of what I am. I am time.

That time is the essence of human existence is fundamental to the existentialist personality theory. It is an insight developed by many philosophers. Among them is Henri Bergson, the French biologically oriented philosopher, who emphasized the importance of time as the underlying phenomenon of all existence, especially biological evolution. Also, of course, the phenomenologist Husserl further developed this idea. Above all, it was Heidegger who made the analysis of time famous as basic to understanding human existence, in his principal work, *Being and Time*. The French existential psychologist Minkowski was one of the first thinkers to apply this notion to psychiatry and psychotherapy. He introduced techniques to diagnose patients by the manner in which they experience time.

I go one step further. I maintain that time is created. The primordial essence, the beginning, the pure consciousness, is prior to time, beyond time, atemporal. It is an Eternal Now.

Part of human existence is temporal. There is another level, however, in which our temporality is *observed*. If we describe the structure of the *observer to time* that we are, then we can no longer think of ourselves in time but must use a category such as the Eternal Now. The relationship here parallels that of Freud's personal and Jung's collective unconscious. These two concepts do not designate conflicting but rather supplementary theories. Jung contends, correctly, in my opinion, that the personal unconscious—having to do with one's specific father and mother—must be worked through and overcome before we can move on to an understanding of the collective unconscious—which concerns the universal archetypes operating in the unexplored and mostly inaccessible part of our personality. In other words, it is not true to say that *I am* my unconscious (individual *or* collective) but that *I observe* my unconscious. This latter act of consciousness dislodges experientially as well as conceptually the inmost center from some of its most intimately cathected objects (objects with which I am identified). Both forms of the unconscious are aspects of the empirical and not the transcendental ego (that is, of the part of me that participates in the world and not that part which is the observer of the world). The empirical ego is the *observed* unconscious. The transcendental ego is the *observer of* the unconscious.

Let us now return to time.

The Constitution of Time

We must return to the discussion in Chapter 10, in which the theory of the constitution of the empirical ego is brought up for the first time. That universal and impersonal act of constitution brings about the individual and personal phenomenon of human finitude. The dynamics of creation have here been termed the archetypal decision for finitude. Although these ideas are controversial, they are on the fulcrum of the issue of finding an answer to death.

Time is created through birth and death. The experience of time appears as a result of the invention of the beliefs in one's personal birth and death. In accepting the reality of death, we become aware that we are time. And to the degree that we perceive ourselves as being time, we are aware of the flow of consciousness that is our nature. Finally, the perception or observation of that pure flow brings into awareness the Eternal Now that is the source of our consciousness. Consciousness, before its state of self-forgetful identification with the empirical or psychological ego—that is, before accepting the beliefs in the birth and death of that ego—is *not* a temporal phenomenon. Consciousness, before it has been conceptually distorted—that is, before constitution and cathexis have taken place—is an atemporal phenomenon, an Eternal Now phenomenon. But once we establish a worldly identity for ourselves, once consciousness confuses itself with the ego—which is isolated, insular, alienated, dies, and is born—it becomes temporal. At that "instant" "I become time."

In older philosophies this theme is the principle of individuation. What is it that plucks you out of the stream of history? What is it that identifies you within the stream of the universe? What *is* your individuality? The answer to these crucial existential questions is that individuation is *the confusion of the cosmic stream of consciousness with an individual object, an empirical or psychological ego.* The sea chooses to think of itself as a fish. Those are the circumstances which create the experience of time.

Therefore, even time—in an absolute, ultimate, final sense—can be considered to be an illusion. The use of the word "illusion" is of course metaphoric. An illusion is an aberration from reality, and the latter must first be defined. At this point in our discussion I mean by reality "pure consciousness"—the most primitive, the irreducible, and the unchanging foundation of Being. But we must not forget that the sense of being an existential individual is also one of the definitions of reality. In the Western tradition, the real-as-universal is often traced to Plato and the Greeks, whereas the notion of the real-as-individual is associated with the Hebrew and Christian traditions. There "Truth" refers to God's specific existential interventions in the world, such as God's pact with Abraham and Jesus' birth.

In other words, time is *created* when we begin to think in terms of birth and death. Or we can state it differently: time and birth-and-death are equivalent concepts and experiences—one leads to the other. As time begins to make sense, birth and death emerge; and as birth and death are understood and accepted, time is created and understood. Birth and death, as conceptual inventions, create time. Time, as a conceptual invention, enables us to use birth and death to define the meaning of a human existence.

It should now be clear that time, constitution, death, and consciousness are interrelated concepts. These are but four words describing four aspects of one complete situation: human existence. Time, constitution, death, and consciousness may well be described as the "four corners of the earth."

BIRTH, DEATH, AND DREAMS AS INVENTIONS

On the basis of the radically empirical approach of phenomenology, the birth and death of the transcendental ego are inventions (or constitutions), because no primary data corresponding to that construct exist or can even be imagined.

The "evidence" for the fact that they are inventions (or constitutions) lies in the fact that such acts may have to be postulated to account for the existence of the concepts of birth and death. Such acts of constitution have the theoretical advantage over the postulation of a dying transcendental ego in that the former can be imagined or conceived, whereas the latter cannot. Futhermore, if one enters deeply enough into meditation, the act of primary constitution (the constitution of the empirical ego) can be actually experienced and carried out.

The effect of that invention (hence, perhaps, also its "purpose") is to create a sense of finite and isolated individuality.

A parallel exists in the area of dreams, which is a theme we have already touched upon in an earlier chapter, and it should be reinforced here. A dream "here and now" is as counterfactual as the experience of the "death-of-myself." A complete phenomenological disclosure of the precise and fringe data and structures that make up a dream shows that a dream is an experience which appears always, or at least most of the time, in the mode of *recollection* or *memory*. But the central philosophical point is that a dream is a good metaphor for the independent reality of the transcendental ego. In this natural analogy the empirical ego is the dream-person and the transcendental ego is the dreamer. From dream to dream the dream-persons change, while the dreamer remains constant. The effect of perceiving the dream phenomenon as a cosmic metaphor is to suggest the eternal in man, the transcendental continuum that runs through human beings. In the applied mythology of world history it becomes the theory of reincarnation. But it is not the individual who is reincarnated, but rather several different individuals (empirical egos) are perceived by one and the same observer (transcendental ego).

We can therefore conclude that, whereas the invention of birth and death is the constitution of finite individuality, the constitution of dreams is the reminder of our transcendental, infinite, and eternal nature. Because that insight is the effect of dreaming, we can say, with depth psychotherapy, that the effect is also the intent. It therefore follows that we as transcendental egos intend and are responsible for the existence of dreams.

The importance of time as an equivalent to human existence itself can be illustrated with the story of John.

"TIME IS OUT OF JOINT"

John's basic problem, as he perceived it, was dual. He was unable to get things done; he felt he did not accomplish or fulfill his goals. Also, he was unable to express his integrity and, consequently, to fight against what he felt were frequent violations of and assaults on his integrity.

He was a teacher, in his early thirties. His wife was also a teacher. They had three relatively young children. Both came from emotionally deprived backgrounds. John had been "intimidated" by life. As a result he said that he tended to perceive all women as mother superiors, a proclivity that makes marriage difficult. He often felt that life took advantage of him and that he could not fight back. His sense of impotence was especially apparent in relations with his wife. She made most of the important decisions in the family. He usually went along with her, but afterwards was angry with himself. He felt *he*, the man, should be the decision maker. For example, true to the spirit of women's liberation, he contributed heavily to the housework. But he then resented his apparent submissiveness and was unable to assert his need for dominance.

His inability to fight back—his general self-concept and life style of impotence and ineffectiveness—was embodied in a high-pitched voice and in a related habit of breathing with his upper chest only. Inside John there was a child who wanted to scream out the truth and solidity of his existence, but could not. The result was actual physical constriction in the upper chest.

When John was encouraged to *really scream*—again and again and again—he lowered and deepened his breathing. We might generalize and say that a constricted voice, a tight chest, and breathing with the upper chest only can be expressions of feeling intimidated, of having been put down, of impotence. As a result, the individual can lose his ability to express himself fully; he cannot feel his energy well up from the base of his torso, his gut, or his pelvis and radiate in waves of power into the world beyond.

John felt guilty and inadequate about the fact that he could never finish what he set out to accomplish. In small tasks he failed himself: the yard work, classroom preparation, organizing his family life. In larger issues he also felt unable to make progress. That category included primarily his career. He seemed tied permanently to a mediocre job; he had little hope of progress, growth, or promotion. His was, in his opinion, a depressing existence.

John had a soft, kind, sweet side and a coarse, rough, hard side. One could see that dichotomy in his face. Sometimes it was mellow, gentle, and warm while at other times it was stolid and jagged like granite. But in his life—in his behavior, in his world—he never manifested or *expressed* that granite side. He built up his life around the self-concept disclosed by the timid, gentle face; but all of a sudden the granite face would come through, and the environment that he created with the gentle exterior would then collapse—and there was no new and corresponding world to replace it.

Not in Charge

As a result of such a dichotomous "being-in-the-world," he felt unable to take charge of his life, to say, "This is *me*. This is my life. *I* am going to lead it; it is not going to be led *for* me, even though now other people control it. For thirty-five years my life has been the working out of my one principle of organization, my one self-concept, which is that other people shall make decisions for me."

One's being-in-the-world is very difficult to change. It is as if John had already built a house and now insisted on changing the plans. And what is more, he demanded immediate results. Of course the effect of such a demand is a collapsed building. This trauma happens when, in the middle of life, a person decides to change his personality. His whole life so far has been ordered by one personality; to change suddenly is to clash with his past. That is one reason why intensive counseling is difficult, and why there is resistance to change. Having constructed a system for thirty-five years makes it almost impossible to create a new one.

The inability to take charge of his life, to grasp his existential freedom, was expressed in John as confusion about time. He had difficulties perceiving time with clarity. He lived by a clock that was not synchronized with the clocks of others. His time was different from the time of those around him. He was marching to the beat of another drummer.

There are several ways he or his counselor could have dealt with this lack of synchronicity. John could have been encouraged to adopt the attitude "To hell with people! You go by your time; I go by mine!" But this declaration of independence was not the solution John wanted; he agreed that his sense of time was inauthentic.

Lethargy

John was lethargic and somewhat overweight. He believed his lethargy resulted from his extra weight. He thought if he could lose fifteen pounds, he would have more energy. But it was unlikely that the fifteen extra pounds meant anything. His lack of energy was more a physical expression of his sense of time than a matter for physiological concern. Therefore, it was apparent that unless he changed his sense of time he could not begin to lose any weight.

What precisely was his sense of time? Most of the time John lived in a kind of a daze. This type of embodiment says, Stop time; I do not want it to move. His time was like a quiet pool rather than a river that flows into the sea or the future. His time had stagnated, was without a ripple. Therefore he was always lethargic. His wife complained about it; he complained about it; his school principal complained about it. I am not saying that people *should* move, that they *should* be active rather than reflective. But when a person comes to a counselor and complains about his apathy, then the counselor should demand, "Accept that; that is your sense of time; you live in a sense of eternity, you are a mystic." Or, "Change that, synchronize your time with world time."

His lethargy was a physical way of expressing the fact that for him time stood still. Another indication of this was the unorthodox way he kept his appointments. John missed one appointment altogether; he did not show up and did not call that day. For the next appointment he appeared forty-five minutes early. There was clearly a considerable time disorientation. In fact, he never carried a watch. He never knew what time it was. He had no adequate sense of whether or not he had the time for what he needed to do.

The Future

A third indication of John's time confusion appeared in his response to questions about how he perceived the future. I asked him to describe himself as he thought he would be ten, twenty, or twenty-five years from now: "Do you have a picture of your future? If not, can you create a picture? Or is that difficult?" These can be revealing questions. John's answer to these inquiries was that nothing will change in the future. "Nothing will change, not even in twenty years from now, nothing will be different: same house, same family set-up. I'll feel the same, I'll have the same kind of relationship with my wife." He was indeed a person for whom time had stood still.

How should the insights of existential philosophy be used to help someone like John change his experience of time? I have argued that time is the most fundamental organizing principle in human existence, and that we invent time. John's archetypal decision was to organize his life in terms of a time that stands still. This means of self-definition is one of the most ancient organizing principles in a person's life. It is more primitive than the Oedipus complex; and it is more difficult to change the mode of experiencing time than to resolve that famous complex. It is easier for an individual to remember his sexual feelings toward his mother or his father, or to develop fantasies about what Freud called the "primal scene," than it is for him to change his way of constituting, organizing, perceiving, and conceptualizing *time*.

Because the constitution of time is connected with the invention of death, I asked John to describe the image of his own death. In response to the question of when he thought he would die, he answered, "At sixty." This means that as of then he felt that his life was more than half over. He believed he had not achieved meaning in his life. It was getting late. This finding was commensurate with the other aspects of his world. There was no temporal movement in his life. And he believed his life would not be different in its second half.

And then I asked him, "How do you think you will die?" He answered, "A heart attack." This was saying that he would die of something *inside* himself—not *outside*. The principle of death was at work within him. *He* was going to do his own dying; *he* was going to be the cause of his own death. This was another way of saying that he was dying already. Perhaps he was dead already. For John, death was an internal phenomenon—a foreign body in him. Not getting anywhere in life is a form of dying. John was dying then and that is far different from understanding *the real meaning of death* in an authentic existence. Thus, when he described himself as a person who would die at 60 of a heart attack, he was also describing himself as one who does not experience himself as the *movement of time into the future.* He had no clear picture of the future; the future was not important, not real, not promising, and not hopeful. I concluded therefore that (a) he could not futurize himself and that (b) the cause was internal.

Change of Time

Now comes the task of the counselor or philosopher. How could John be helped to change his sense of time? Two existential themes applied to John: the idea that his self-concept was self-constituted, and the idea that his awareness of his death clarified for him the structure of an authentic existence. Maybe he could be helped to create a self-image that would change his unhealthy experience of time. And his idea of his own death might give him the clue of how to change to that new self-image. He needed an "existential prescription." In his case, it had a quick effect.

A philosophically oriented counselor might have spoken as follows to John: "You need a new self-image. You need a new concept, a new idea, a new principle around which your idea of what you are can be organized. Let me suggest something. Let us take our clue from what you now think you are. Your experience of time is compressed in the image of your death, which is that of a person who at 60 will die of a heart attack. Therefore, if we can *change* your image of your death, we might also change your perception of time. Consequently, rather than to tackle the time problem directly, let us tackle it by changing the concept of your own death."

The counselor might continue: "Make the effort to think of yourself as dying not at 60 but at 95. Imagine yourself to be a 95-year-old man. Look around at 95-year-old men. Think of the late Pablo Casals. Or of Picasso or Bertrand Russell. These are—or were—models we can use. Think of yourself as a 95-year-old man.

"Now make another major change in your death concept. Think of yourself not as dying from a heart attack, but from an external cause or force, such as an airplane crash. You achieve in this way a new self-concept. If you die of a heart attack, then the principle of death is within you. In the end it catches up with you. Death is becoming what you are; death fulfills your destiny. But if you die in an airplane crash, then you die too young. Even if you die at 95, in an airplane crash, you die in the prime of life. You could have lived longer. In this case you carry within you the principle of life, of time, of movement, of process, of self-transcendence, of creativity, of evolution.

"Remember that the person who dies of a heart attack carries the principle of his demise within him. The person who is shot or is killed in a car accident or in an airplane crash does *not* carry the principle of death within him; he is the principle of eternal life. Only because of some stupid external accident his life is snuffed out.

"By changing your self-image from a 60-year-old man dying from a heart attack to a 95-year-old man dying in an airplane crash, the fundamental organizing principle in your life, the most ancestral organizing principle in your life, that archetypal decision which creates your sense of time, your experience of futurity, will undergo a radical change."

And it did. It was not very difficult for John to keep in mind that new self-image. Identifying himself feelingly and experientially with a 95-year-old man who would die in an airplane crash facilitated a change in the foundation structure of his world view. Furthermore, John made a deliberate effort to focus his thoughts on time. It was suggested to him, "Think of this afternoon, think of it in terms of one o'clock, two o'clock, three, four, and five o'clock. Now it is ten o'clock, and all the other hours follow in order. Think of this afternoon in terms of numbers."

This conceptualization of time was something he had had difficulties with before. He had not thought of time in that sense. In the past, he would just drift into the afternoon and suddenly an appointment or some other obligation would catch up with him and he would exclaim, "My goodness, I don't have any time left!"

When he became accustomed to this new self-image (i.e., death-image) a changed sense of time emerged in him. He started thinking in terms of specific units of time. He began to think about tomorrow: morning, noon, afternoon, evening. It was further suggested to him that he "start thinking in terms of each day of the week: Monday, Tuesday, Wednesday, Thursday, Friday, Saturday, Sunday. Then in terms of a month: the first, second, third of the month, and so on. What day of the month is today? Then think in terms of seasons. Now is summer; what will happen in the fall? Now think in terms of years.

"Finally, can you now answer with a clear image the question, What will your life be like in twenty-five years?"

John was re-trained to reconstitute his sense of time so that his experience is now futurized. In this way his problem of finding meaning in life and of reconstructing his personality is on the way to solution. This approach to human fulfillment is no less effective for not being dramatic. What matters in this case is continuity and support.

In this particular situation this philosophical approach worked very well. In another situation it might be totally irrelevant. These techniques must be adapted to individual circumstances.

Nothing permanent is accomplished by merely introducing an idea. However, the right idea leads to change and movement in a person's life; it results not only in small change, but yields fundamental change. If a person changes his perception of time, he is making as fundamental a change as is possible. Such a change is even more fundamental than a change of sex—although less dramatic and obvious.

Once an idea works you can preserve it and you build on it. John's story seemed worth sharing because it serves as a practical and useful example of how the concept of death works therapeutically by affecting the individual's sense of time.

I shall conclude this part on the structure of consciousness by spelling out in detail how the notion of individuality—the existential "standing out" of a personality from his background—emerges from the universal and impersonal sea of transcendental cousciousness that courses through us. The exposition of the structure of that consciousness and its experiential accessibility to us has been the principal topic in Part Three of this analysis of death.

16

The Creation
of the Individual

TIME AND ANXIETY

I always search for a simple formula that will compress the natural law metaphysics which I call the existential personality theory into a few words or sentences. The usefulness of such a formula lies in its potential for reconstructing the personality. By keeping in mind this formula we can eliminate distortions and learn to see Being as it is; we can therefore be helped to lead a "natural" life—that is, a life consonant with the deepest philosophically revealed structure of Being. A key concept in human development in general and in psychotherapy in particular is that of the *identity* of the individual. The question of how the sense of individuality is brought about is the base on which all thought about mental health is balanced. It is in this problem area where a philosophical discussion of death and immorality, of the individual and the cosmic, of the nature of consciousness and its relation to the world, can aid in fundamental clarification. Because we assume responsibility for being individuals and having an identity, we talk in terms of inventing or creating this all-important sense of individuality.

The key concepts in the creation of the individual are *time* and *anxiety*. We have already discussed the hypothesis that the constitution of birth and death[1] create the experience of time. Time—that is, the sense that we are temporal and thus history-creating beings—is expressed in daily life as responsibility, dependability, and consistency.

---

[1] Note the absence of the subject, "ego," or "I" in the way in which the creation of the individual is phrased. "I create myself into an individual" does not make sense, because the "I" precedes the "individual," making that creation really a duplication. "An individual is created" or "consciousness creates itself into an alienated individual" are

These traits therefore become the hallmarks of a successfully developed *individual*. These manifestations of time—because they deal with consequences—express the intentional *continuity* of subject with world or object, a continuity that is, according to Heidegger, a mostly temporal phenomenon.

The world is organized by consciousness into patterns, objects, substances, processes, and values. Phenomenology calls this process of world view construction, "constitution." When we start philosophizing, we find that these constitutions already are there for us. But this process can be reversed, through "deconstitution," which makes possible the deep changes in personality available through intensive psychotherapy. These changes we call reconstitutions. The pure consciousness, the transcendental ego, behind these foundation activities—a center accessible through intensive and courageous deconstitution—leads to the sense of impersonal immortality and is properly called the Eternal Now.

The relation between the experience of anxiety and the sense of individuality is more complex. Anxiety means, in part, alienation. As the world recedes, the individual, alone, is created. To be an individual means not to be the world, to be an alien in the world. Freud expressed beautifully this philosophical truth in the Oedipus metaphor. A person who marries a replica of a parent or who cannot connect love and sex still responds to all persons as if they were his parents. He who cannot relate to another as a person, but for whom closeness always and immediately means hetero- and homosexuality, still relates to persons as if they were his parents. This fragmentation or dichotomy can be explained as follows: If a parent is experienced sexually, then he cannot be faced spiritually or in love. Similarly, if the child is close to his parent spiritually—that is, in love—he cannot envisage any sexual possibilities. It is the child who is expected to fragment physical and spiritual closeness, and it should not come as a surprise if as an adult he finds it difficult to establish integration.

But why should an individual persist in projecting his parents on all the persons he meets? The answer is that he cannot give up the archetype of a parent, which is his symbol of a totally secure tie to all Being. A child in infancy is secure because he rests, unalienated, in the bosom of Being. However, he begins to feel the anxiety of his aloneness (he begins to repress, have dreams and nightmares) when he dis-

---

the only meaningful statements we can make, because we are dealing here with the most primitive material that exists in the structure of personality. We are concerned with the condition of *being* preceding the sense of *being an individual*.

covers that his parents are not God. They are human and they are beginning to fail him as surrogates for the plenitude of Being. And with
the appearance of each new imperfection he gets another blow for
alienation with ensuing separation anxiety. Eventually he learns that
his parents are mortal: One day their abandonment and his separation
will be total. That separation, which is really separation from God, is
experienced correctly as a split in Being itself. Parents are empirical
symbols for a transcendental reality. To the growing child, the external world becomes a void, pure nothingness. He is slowly forced to
make the philosophical discovery that as an individual he stands alone
in the cold and dark of empty space. He has now reached the stage of
personality development in which the world has been negated. And
this is the manner in which anxiety gives rise to the sense of individuality. He who resists this extraordinary and painful growth to mature
individuality will compulsively invent his parents all over again by projecting their archetypal image on all he meets. He will rediscover his
parents in lovers, friends, models, teachers, bosses, and leaders. He
cannot let go of them because he has never understood or learned the
meaning of being an individual.

The mature individual, on the other hand, will destroy or resolutely
face the abandonment of these parental archetypes and confront the
existential loneliness of the chooser and self-definer that he in fact is.
He is then ready to meet both males and females as persons and not
as sexual objects. He has blossomed into full human individuality.

I call this complex and exceptionally important process the *decision
for finitude*. It is the existential *ground* as presented by Kirkegaard,
Nietzsche, and Heidegger. It is the concreteness of Rollo May's I-am
experience in which I understand what it means and how it feels to
take responsibility for being myself. That is the experience of the core.
And we must find ways—didactic, intellectual, emotional, and experiential—to facilitate achieving this realization.

THE CORE

When, as a child, I first went to Caracas, Venezuela, in 1937, I was
struck by what appeared to be houses but were facades only. The
fronts, brick structures with doors and windows, had no backs. They
hid cardboard shanties. Some people are like that: pure front, role,
cover, facade, or *persona*. Let us call these individuals, "front-only persons." When, much later, I had occasion to visit the Kasbah in Mo-

rocco, I remember a humble and rundown front, behind which was a richly appointed Sultan's palace, complete with resplendent mosaics and sparkling fountains. Some people are like that: modest in front, but with great, exciting, and beautiful depth. Let us call these individuals, "front-and-depth persons."

The former persons have flat affect, the latter can have deep and genuine feelings. The former neither understand nor make commitments, the latter are richly identified with what is important and worthy. The former are dull, the latter exciting. The former copy the values around them, the latter are inner-directed.

Lila, a 31-year-old woman, was a front-only person. Whenever I asked her how she *felt*, what she experienced *now*, or what sensations she was having in her *body*, her response was always the same, "I don't understand what you mean." She had no real father. I asked her, "Imagine that you can recreate and relive your childhood; what kind of father would you invent?" Her answer was, "One whom I can respect, one who has parties and friends, and one who is strong and reliable." I gave her a chance to reflect: "Anything else you want in a father?" After some thought she said, "No, nothing; that's all."

It seems a pity that there was one quality she had neglected. She did not say, "I want a father who loves me unconditionally and who has made an absolute and lifelong commitment to me!"

Perhaps it is legitimate to infer that the love and commitment of a father encourages the development of the depth and three-dimensionality that we cherish in the human character: the core. It may be that the mother, as a type rather than as a unique person, encourages the development of intimacy. Lila was a person who did not have much of a "presence" (a favorite word with Gabriel Marcel). She did not seem "real" in that her feelings were "flat." She was a "dissociated" person, a front-only individual. Let us now turn our attention to the other, more real type of person.

What precisely is it we experience when we meet a front-and-depth person? The individual in question is real and exciting; the person is full of life. The front-and-depth person is often anxious and a lot of feelings seem to be just beneath the surface. This person is apt to be exciting and attractive, poetic, romantic, and creative, but also a bit frightening. In that person one experiences what I like to call the "creative erotic energy core." This concept is a phenomenological description of what one experiences in meeting such a human being.

What you feel when you meet a front-and-depth person is the hard nodule or condensation of individuality at the center of that person. In counseling, if that core is not present, it is the responsibility of the counselor to elicit it, to create a safe and welcoming environment for it. The core must be challenged through confrontation, otherwise only rarely is it born. In the case of the anxious individual, in whom the core is present but timid and fearful, the person must be assisted to give full birth and expression to that sprouting core. Birth without destructive explosiveness is the prescription. By using such words as "hard," "core," "energy," "creative," "erotic," "nodule," and "condensation," I hope to present an evocative description of one of the crucial messages of existentialism: the sense of being an authentic, individual *Existenz*, which is Jaspers' word for this core.

The meaning of this core, the significance of developing it fully, cannot be measured out in psychological terms alone. After psychology comes philosophy. A thoroughly analyzed person, or one who has successfully completed a program of intensive depth psychotherapy, has transcended psychology and has become a creative and fulfilled person—an artist, philosopher, poet, musician, novelist, sportsman, reformer, etc. Creativity is the ultimate condition of health. And to be creative is the role of the artist. After psychology comes art. No one can be philosophically healthy unless he thinks of himself as creative or artistic. It must be understood, however, that artistic creativity can be expressed in *any* worldly activity whatever, from painting to business, from poetry to automobile mechanics, and from music to politics. An act is creative by virtue of the mode in which it is performed and not because of appearances.

The aesthetic and mystical genius now becomes the conscience of the healed individual. Nothing but creativity will satisfy him anymore. Anytime he is not creative, but is instead tempted to be satisfied with mediocrity, his conscience will bother him. The decision to become an adult means not reason and civility, practicality and forebearance, but the choice to become the profound and creative artist that is the philosophic consciousness lurking in the shadows of the unconscious of us all. This is the dimension of depth that personalized education in philosophy can contribute to psychotherapy, because therapy that does not invoke the conscience of the creative artist in us may serve as anodyne, but is not a true healing.

The creative-erotic energy core requires additional phenomenological description, because this concept is meant to evoke a feeling for the "hardness" and "substantiality" that is involved in the creation of an existing individual. The creative-erotic energy core can be individualistic, but it can also be intimate or social, in the sense that for some, love or identification with a society provides identity. Consciousness comes in many modes. Some people are mavericks, others lovers, and still others gregarious. The creative-erotic energy core is related to what I call the first of the modes of consciousness—that is, consciousness as individualistic.[2] That Level is prerequisite for establishing the second level, consciousness as intimacy, intersubjectivity, or as loving encounter.

But there is a third type of consciousness, the "social consciousness." That is the kind of consciousness which thinks in social, group, tribal, or national terms. We do not have much representation of that consciousness in the individualistic West. It is characteristic of oriental and African nations, where the family, tribal, national, and/or cultural consciousness is the dominant experience. It is the kibbutz experience in Israel and the suicidal fanaticism, born of despair, of the Palestinians. That consciousness helps man identify himself with the desperate vicissitudes of the world today, including starvation around the globe of ten million of more children a year. Such staggering facts lead away from thinking of oneself as an individual and lead toward thinking of the human race as a single and progressively evolving entity.

Core Dreams

In my effort to develop a phenomenology of the creative-erotic energy core, I have come across dreams which illustrate the authentic constitution of the individual. The dreams I shall discuss briefly are about selected problems in the constitution of the individual involved. In each life these problems are different. Nevertheless, in order to understand the foundation on which most psychotherapy rests, we must make progress in philosophy regarding the *constitution of the individual.*

Larry

Larry, a man of 30, and exceptionally gifted in philosophical, literary, and poetic matters, had a couple of puzzling and troublesome dreams.

One dream had a game quality to it. He was with people who were discussing matters of great interest to them, but whom he could not understand. He felt a wall between them. He took a gun and shot

[2] *Managing Anxiety* (Englewood Cliffs, N.J.: Prentice-Hall, 1974), Master Table, Item A2a.

himself, after which he slid over to these whispering people, through the wall. On the other side he felt peace and excitement, and he became strangely convinced that an important decision had been made.

While dead, and just before sliding over, a former girl-friend appeared from the rear left (the "sinister" shadow side); he turned toward her and warmly embraced her, feeling a glow of excitement that was not exactly sexual in nature. Then the girl melted fully with him.

In a later dream, he was looking for a script he could not find. He needed it for the play in which he was to perform. Two women, one dressed in red and one in black (a Hallowe'en witch) offered to find it for him.

The game and play quality of both dreams may indicate that Larry's world design was *the inability to make commitments.* In actual fact, the absence of commitment characterized most aspects of Larry's life: he could not make a commitment to wife, children, job, education, etc. He felt great guilt for neglecting his talents, which meant he could not make a commitment even to himself.

His two dreams told him:

1. He must destroy (shoot) his noncommitted (alienated) self before he could experience his creative-erotic energy core. What were the people saying, and what did he have to destroy to hear them? His core was the people who said what in truth he wanted to say but whom he—as the alienated self—could not understand. In real life, the alienation from his essence, from his core, gave him an empty feeling of separation and loneliness. His loneliness could not be relieved by more of the same old medicine: a better job, more education, new women, etc. His loneliness was *self*-estrangement, loss of his core; it was that alienation which had to be overcome.

2. He needed to contact the feminine in him. Woman meant to him the creative, the fulfilling, but also passion (red) and danger (black witch). In other words, woman, whom he must embrace and merge with before he could destroy his present self to give birth to the self that was in touch with the unconscious, was the demonic aspect (passion) of the creative core within him.

Larry was to be understood not in terms of psychopathology, but in terms of Kierkegaard and Nietzsche, Beethoven and Chopin. He was a "European" mind: His field of consciousness was not social (middle class), cosmic (oriental mysticism, flower children), or objective (the scientific community). He was romantic (the individual consciousness, the demonic genius, the creative-erotic energy core), misplaced in age, culture, and continent.

The only help a philosopher could offer him was to point out his *resistances* to a commitment to romanticism, because the latter was his destiny, curse, karma, or fate, a concept the Greeks called *Moira*. But that was the commitment he could not make; his superego was still punishing him with middle-class lifestyles. And the society around him, including the medical and therapeutic communities, were strictly anti-romantic. However, once the need for that bohemian-artistic commitment became clear and it was finally made, he felt whole. Having touched his core, even a middle-class commitment, if he so chooses, is now within the realm of his authentic possibilities.

Gordon

One further dream clarifies the notion of the creative-erotic energy core. Gordon dreamed he was wrestling with an enormous and poisonous snake. In the dream he felt the snake was his father. He managed to cut it in half and its poison dripped from its fangs all over his hands. At this, he experienced a great sense of resolution, joy, and peace.

There are numerous possible interpretations that suggest themselves. All, I believe, add up to the same meaning. Here are a few: In a Freudian context we can say he cut off his father's penis, whose sperm (power) was poisonous to him. In a Jungian context we can argue that he resisted or destroyed seduction (Eve and the snake in the Garden of Eden myth). Or perhaps he castrated himself because for him manhood or creativity are poisonous, dangerous, and self-destructive.

All these possibilities (and more) add up, in my opinion, to the following existential assessment: In the dream Gordon destroyed his father, which means he acquired personal independence and integrity. And that was a fundamental resolution in his life. In real life, he gave up the business he had been in and the marriage which he discovered represented his father's values, decisions, and instructions. He was no longer to be seduced by them, as he had been bribed in the past. The result was a sense of peace, wholeness, rightness, and resolution. In addition, he was now in touch with his essence, his creative core; and, as with Larry, that creativity has its share of the demonic. I have in my office an artist's conception of a volcanic Beethoven erupting in a cloud of thunder and lightning to remind my students of this romantic and individualistic point.

An analysis of freedom and of decision making also can lead us to the sense of being an individual—that is, to the experience of the creative-erotic energy core.

SAYING "NO"

The creation of an individual can be facilitated when an existential counselor helps people make difficult decisions *during the limits of the counseling hour.* These immediate and mini-decisions have the larger meaning of choices-to-be-yourself or general self-definitions. The decision made in the counseling hour is like a small button to which is attached the power that turns irreversibly the giant tanker. The button is depressed in the counseling hour and the tanker turns in the outside life. A pearl is patiently built by the oyster, layer upon layer. The core is built up through layers of decisions. Here are a few examples.

Joan

Joan, a woman in her twenties, loved her brother, who was about to enter a marriage she considered disastrous. She *must* attend the wedding ceremony to preserve her relationship with her brother. She eventually interpreted the meaning (*to her*) of that decision to be the following: "My integrity or authenticity does not want me to go. Going would mean I accept my brother's symbolic death. However, not going—and he may never speak to me again—means I respect his true nature, his integrity, and his authenticity. Not to attend his wedding would be for me an act of genuine concern and love—especially if I made clear to him exactly why I am not going and explained how difficult the decision was for me." In the counseling hour, Joan was challenged to make a decision for being herself rather than, as she had been used to, against herself. Afterward, it would be merely a question of whether or not she was to continue making the decision she knew was the authentic one for her.

After coming to understand the decision regarding her brother's wedding and realizing that the decision was made right then in the office, Joan did not return for more counseling. However, she did send the following letter about two months later, indicating, I believe, that the decision to be an individual (the "I-am" experience, the core) had been attained by her.

Thank you so much for your help. I'm feeling much stronger, like I've come home to myself, and can trust myself once again. It's a good feeling. The freedom which I tried to exchange for security when I got married, and my integrity, both of these have been returned to me, and these are certainly the greatest gifts. I am also realizing that I must not be afraid to be myself, even though being a strong and relatively independent woman brings many reprisals in larger society. Of course, I have far to go, and much work to do, I don't delude myself about that. But with your help I have managed to cross the fence, to bridge the critical gap. I am very grateful.

I want to tell you that today as I was walking on campus, a feeling welled up inside me, and I experienced the world differently than I ever have before. I felt a oneness with everyone around me; it's so subtle it's hard to describe; but I didn't feel isolated. I felt like a participant in a stream of consciousness which links everyone together. And the feeling didn't go away, it stayed with me, and I relaxed, like letting go with a deep sigh. My relationships with my friends and co-workers were different. Even this evening at work I was able to evoke this feeling, and sort of consciously let go of my ego. I feel very warm and happy about this, and at the same time scared that it'll go away. I'm growing very fast now, every day is a new day. I'm able to evoke this new feeling at will. You have truly done a remarkable thing for me.

Bob

Bob, a man in his early thirties, was still a child. He used several devices to defend himself against growing up. It was difficult for him to make the decision of taking responsibility for being himself. In one counseling session, he mentioned casually that his parents were coming to visit. "Do you want them to come?" I asked. "No!" was his peremptory reply. I suggested that he make a difficult and important call: "Tell them that you are in the process of working out some of unfinished childhood business and that the present time is not a good one for the three of you to get together." "But I have not told them that I am seeing you for philosophic counseling," he responded. "Would you like them to know, or is this a matter you wish to keep private?" I asked. His answer was quick: "I very much want them to know, but I am embarrassed. They will think I am weak." "Well," I continued, "tell them in the same call that you feel very good about having entered into a philosophic counseling relationship."

Sometimes, in order to give the person added support to make an authentic decision I ask him to call me afterward and tell me how it went. I also reassure him—because I believe it to be true and because everyone needs hope—that he will find the world responsive to his decision. In addition, I give him tools to prevent explosive reactions and to handle them if they should occur.

Kay

Kay's problem is another illustration of the connection between decision making and the creative-erotic energy core. It also shows how confronting a student or client with a now-decision—to be carried out during the counseling hour (such as a phone call, a written statement, a contract, another appointment, a cancellation, or terminating the relationship)—can lead to the creation of the all-important sense of individuality.

Kay was a very anxious and bright 24-year-old woman whose marriage was a constant series of volcanic eruptions. Her anxiety and the urgency with which she wanted to make an appointment for her husband were devices she used to prevent making the decision to be herself, to take responsibility for being herself, to be in touch with her core. Her anxiety prevented discussion, and her desire for an appointment for her husband indicated that she wanted him to do her work. (This is not to deny either that her anxiety was genuine or that her husband had problems.) Her anxiety was the uncontrollable experience that she needed to say "I am," and be heard in so speaking. Her anxiety was *fear* of being herself and *anger* at her self-betrayal for not being herself.

As I have indicated earlier, some anxious persons are much more real than those with flat affect. Their anxiety is their reality. It insures that their inner erotic and creative energy core can be directly perceived by others. These anxious persons are not alienated in the schizoid sense, as would be persons with no feelings at all.

Kay said that she revealed all her secrets to her husband. She also volunteered that she was unable to achieve an orgasm in sex. A philosophic analysis of these two facts was that to make the decision to be herself required a zone of privacy. Because she told her husband all, the only privacy she reserved for herself was the orgasm, which she then—and rightly so—refused to relinquish. That refusal was not a sexual malfunction but an authentic choice for a zone of privacy. During the counseling hour she made the following *now*-decisions: Her husband, she said, was waiting at home with bated breath to find out what happened in counseling. She decided to speak to him as follows: "In my session I was working on *our* marriage. I feel that it may be more constructive for *our* marriage if for the time being you and I do not discuss some of these issues." Furthermore, she would from now on keep her private correspondence private. The "no" with which she determined to insure her privacy is clear. But it is stated gently, respectfully, and compassionately. It is both effective and kind, which means it is mature.

It was important to pin her down so that she could experience clearly that decision making is unavoidable. It is this inevitability that creates the individual core. I therefore told her to gauge *her commitment to herself* by her effectiveness in (1) maintaining her privacy and (2) not threatening her husband. She now had a club and it might have been tempting to hit him with it. But such aggression would only have reflected her own lack of self-respect.

It took Kay's husband three days to get used to her new freedom, centeredness, privacy, and independence. Kay was very insistent that her counseling, which really contained no special secrets, not be discussed at home. She came to see me a week later, proud and relaxed. "Never before have I been as proud of myself," she said, "as I was this week, when I stood up for my right to privacy. What is more, I lost my anxiety."

This discussion leads to a few generalizations.

I find it useful in almost all cases of philosophic counseling to assume that the individual is angry and contemptuous at his inner weakness—which is mostly an ontological rather than a pathological condition—and as a result does not function or cope well either in his own fulfillment (where he lacks energy, achievement, and direction) or in encounters (he is angry and hostile toward people who make themselves vulnerable to his aggression by offering him love). Inner weakness and self-contempt express themselves as a failure of the will, depression, lack of ambition, ennui, neurasthenia, flatness of affect, and lack of *joie de vivre*. Such an individual is dependent; he (or she) *wants to be taken care of* (this can be true of both men and women). For example, a woman may be ambitious, self-affirming, and individualistic. . . until a man comes along who, she thinks, will take care of her. Instantly all ambition wanes. Will such a marriage work? No. She will always resent her weakness and take it out on him.

Does this analysis suggest some generalized answers? Yes: Therapists should develop techniques to bring about a confrontation—within the general context of a transcendental relationship, that is, a common-contact field of two conscious centers who together examine and share the personal growth of the client. The latter must have been established through a long period of trust. And it is this confrontation, within an atmosphere of acceptance, that can bring about the creation of the individual.

GUILT AND ANXIETY

The management of guilt and anxiety depends on the existence of the creative-erotic energy core. But it is also true that the more experience were get in managing guilt and anxiety the more firm will be our ego core. Let us consider a final example.

Don

Don chose to leave his wife and children for another woman, Claudia. The decision was mature, in that it was made after much agony and deliberation and it was made in the direction of growth. He came to me complaining of considerable anxiety and intense guilt. Yet he knew that the decision to leave his family and to move in the direction of Claudia and a new life was right for him and, in a manner of speaking, inevitable. Our work together had moved from (a) the attempt to reconcile the marriage, to (b) his decision to leave the marriage, to (c) his quest for meaning in his life (he was preparing himself emotionally for a second career), to, finally, (d) severe guilt and some anxiety about the decision undertaken.

Following is a schematic outline of my response. It illustrates the existential way of managing the guilt and anxiety of decision making as a prelude for the experience of the core.

1. *You are going through a critical point (Kairos, Tillich called it) in your life.* In fact, this may be the conversion and the transformation to the new self and the new life that was meant to be. This may be the transition to fulfillment that had to come before death will remove life from you forever.

2. *This decision may be the first real decision you have ever made.* A decision is real if it is impossible to make it on ordinary terms. A decision is real if no amount of reason, calculation, and option analysis seems to make any difference.

3. *I fully share the depth of your agony.* I am with you in your pain and shall see you through to the end, regardless of what your decisions will be. In fact, to accentuate the reality of our encounter, our transcendental relationship, the common intersubjective field we have established, I will share with you some of my own experiences in the area of decision making. I will risk sharing with you some of my intimate agony, thereby expressing my equality with you, my faith in you,

and punctuating the burden of your independence to you.[3] (By sharing with the patient, the counselor recognizes that the former is also an adult. This challenges and confronts him.)

4. *Not only are you now making a decision about your marriage, but your decision also has the cosmic character of creation; you are defining a new self, a new life, a new moral code, and a new idea of man.* Your problem is not a form of mental illness, but it is a normal and healthy issue in life and philosophy. In fact, you are on the threshhold of reaching philosophic insight and depth worthy of the most distinguished thinkers and creators in history.

5. *Do not delude yourself into believing that guilt and anxiety can or should be avoided.* No pill or technique is relevant. Your anxiety and guilt are *real.* They are perceptions of the truth. People *are* being hurt, and it is your decision that is hurting them. The project that intends to avoid anxiety and guilt is the inauthentic project of destroying your humanity and the accomplishments of your character growth. To avoid the guilt and anxiety of decision making at this point would undo all the achievements that our work together has accomplished.

6. *You have reached the level of life in which you recognize its seriousness.* Young cultures are naive, inexperienced, and flippant. Old cultures tend to be wise and serious. Life is serious and you have made that discovery. Happiness, joy, play, all these are meaningful and delightful; but they are empty to anyone who is not in touch with the dimensions of seriousness and of tragedy that are also present in human existence.

7. *Any authentic decision contains guilt and anxiety.* Regardless of how you choose, values will be destroyed. In your case—and each case is analyzed individually—remaining in your marriage would lead to the equal guilt and anxiety of unfulfilled potential, of inexcusable self-denial, weakness, and worthlessness.

8. *You have now joined the small and exclusive circle of adults.* Up to now, not having made *real* decisions, you have been a child. Now you are an adult. You now have the experience of standing alone. You want answers, and none are forthcoming; you want help, and no one can give it to you. You want support, and in truth you are in a vacuum. All a counselor or friend can do is to share, in love, that aloneness with

---

[3] This situation can be illustrated with an imaginary telephone conversation in a suicide prevention center in which eventually the volunteer pours out his problems on the caller! In that way, the therapist recognizes—in action rather than words—the potential for health, strength, and authenticity of the patient. We must always remember that healing occurs in relationship.

you. The real experience of the creative-erotic energy core that results from decision making is what I call the "authentication of anxiety and guilt."

9. *The experience of man's aloneness is an ontological revelation of the structure of being.* Aloneness, if experienced in truth and with clarity, is the despair of anxiety and guilt. It is the experience of groundlessness and the regret over not conquering it. Weep with the guilt and suffer with the anxiety. I will share those experiences, perceptions, and feelings with you. If you repress or deny your anxiety and guilt, you will develop symptoms: either physical ones, wherever the weakest link happens to be in the chain of your bodily processes, or philosphical ones such as depression, meaninglessness, unloving relationships, self-hate, etc.

In confronting these experiences (anxiety and guilt) you will witness a miracle: the creation of an authentic individual, the experience of the core: You. The fog of anxiety and guilt will gradually condense, congeal, and solidify itself into the concrete experience of a self. Do not waste the guilt and anxiety. A cloud in space congeals over time to produce the hard nodule of a star. The cloud is the anxiety and guilt—the interstellar raw material for the creation of the star. If you deny the guilt and the anxiety you destroy the substance out of which your integrity can be fashioned. If you accept them, you will feel concrete, real, and grounded. A new you will have been born. It is a you that is at peace and that is strong; a you that can choose and live, and a you capable of enormous joy and transcending dignity. You have now come home.

10. *You will now find meaning in life.* One of the tasks we worked on was the search for meaning in the sense of a second career. We had made no progress until our work turned to the guilt. Resolving the guilt in this existential fashion "solved" not only the problem with the divorce but also the larger issue of meaning in you. The ground which you have now discovered is also the creative source of your meaning.

These points cover the existential "strategy." One issue remains, and it has to do with respect for the future. The core is tempered by anticipating the blows of the future and by seeing a permanent place for it under the sun. The patient must be given honest hope.

11. *Think now of the future. Share these experiences in love.* Share your insights, feelings, experiences, and perceptions with your new love. *Entrust, for the first time in your life, your weaknesses to a woman.* You have been an unusually healthy and strong man who has never depended on anyone. Your weaknesses have been deeply buried. Sharing them

may have the same conversion effect as did the congealing of your guilt and anxiety. Later, you will be able to reconstruct your relationships with your children by equally trusting them with the richness, fullness, and agony of your total experience. Children can understand philosophy at any age.

RESISTANCE TO IMMORTALITY

The experience of being an individual develops out of the experiences of anxiety and pure consciousness. At the end of this book are some so-called "immortality exercises," which I have used with my students. These innocuous-sounding exercises are often resisted, however. And that very opposition is the struggle to protect their individuality.

These exercises (Chapter 19), when I read them to my students, have a trancelike effect. Responses to them are primarily of peace and relaxation; the general level of anxiety is considerably relieved. But the negative resistance, which takes some prodding to be revealed, is exhibited in anxiety, rebellion, or repulsion. Such feelings represent *fear of, anger at,* and *resistance to the surrender to cosmic consciousness.*

This anxiety or anger is an important counseling tool. It amounts to one experience: premonition *and* avoidance of the experience of cosmic oneness. If we now use the word "anxiety" to describe the totality of this negative response, then we discover that *this experience of anxiety is the actual experience of making the choice to be an individual.* The fundamental decision in the whole spectrum of an existential-phenomenological metaphysics is the "decision for finitude," "taking responsibility for the burden of being myself," "the decision for being," "the I-am experience," etc. Other names for the *results* of that archetypal decision are "uniqueness," "individuality," "centeredness," "resoluteness," "courage," "authenticity," "self-actualization," etc. That is the experience of the creative-erotic energy core. It is the foundation for understanding the meaning of being an individual. It is my view that the anxiety aroused by these immortality exercises is the actual experience of choosing finitude over divinity; it is the actual experience of choosing humanity over the transpersonal, the temporal over the eternal, the individual over the cosmic, the particular over the universal.

The decision to be a finite, existing, individual core is an *ex nihilo* decision, one that can only be made from the depth of the nothingness that we are. Understandably, we resist this insight because once our freedom for universality is made clear to us we may not choose to return to our individuality.

In sum, to experience resistance against the immortality exercises is *to experience the actual creation of the individual in the sea of cosmic consciousness* which in meditation we experience ourselves to be (and which in religion is called God). This creation is the most important decision in the universe but it is, at the same time, based on nothing at all. Thus, this experience of anxiety is the experience of the birth of the ego or the decision that gives birth to the ego. And resistance to the immortality exercise is the fierce rebellion against the surrender and destruction of the ego.

We see once more that anxiety is not an emotion but a state of cognition and revelation. Anxiety, by disclosing to us our freedom and our nothingness as the essential foundations of our existence, leads us to experience our individual center and puts us in touch with our creative source. To develop this theme is the first task of all therapy and is specifically the goal of personalized education in philosophy.

REMEMBER

1. Consciousness is different from the objects of consciousness (Chapter 12).
2. Every object is part consciousness (Chapter 12).
3. Every consciousness is part object (Chapter 12).
4. Consciousness and the world are continuous with one another (Chapter 12).
5. Consciousness is nonpositional (Chapter 13).
   a. Consciousness is not in the person (Chapter 13).
   b. Consciousness is not in the world (Chapter 13).
6. A cosmic consciousness runs through me (Chapter 13).
7. The active consciousness participates in the world (Chapter 14).
8. The passive consciousness is eternal (Chapter 14).
9. Birth and death are transcendental inventions (Chapter 14).
10. The constitution of birth and death create the sense of finite individuality (Chapter 14).
11. I am time (Chapter 15).
12. The *observation* of time is the experience of pure *consciousness* as the Eternal Now (Chapter 15).
13. The constitution of birth and death create the sense of time (Chapter 15).

14. Dreams are constituted as reminders of our transcendental nature (Chapter 15).
15. The sense of individuality is the experience of the creative-erotic energy core (Chapter 16).
16. Meaning is found in the lifestyle of the artist-philosopher (Chapter 16).
17. Decision making produces the sense of being an individual (Chapter 16).
18. As individuals, we resist the surrender to pure consciousness (Chapter 16).

Exercises

1. Relaxation facilitates the experience of pure consciousness (Chapter 13).
   a. Feel heavy.
   b. Feel warm.
   c. Feel like a rag doll.
   d. Cover eyes to look inward.
2. Observe your breathing to experience pure consciousness (Chapter 13).

Now that we have developed the idea and the experience of pure consciousness, I shall attempt to delineate how this idea can lead to both a conception and an experience of immortality as one fundamental answer to death.

PART FOUR

IMMORTALITY
AND
THE INDIVIDUAL

17

The Experience of Immortality

If we are going to deal with the answer to death we must face the issue of immortality. Transcendental phenomenology, the description not of objects but of our *consciousness* of objects and the *source* of our consciousness of objects, is the crucial methodology for analyzing possible answers to death.

The theme of this book has been that death reveals the philosophic mysteries of human existence. We therefore are ready for the final revelation, the destruction of death itself. The discovery that can be achieved through focusing on death is the insight into immortality—the eternity of consciousness. No one can deny that "people die." That is an event in the empirical and constituted world. It occurs in the consensual world in which we all live. It is a belief we must accept to be bona fide members of any social order. However, this view of the ego or the individual as ultimate is not an axiom of existence but an archetypal belief system organized by the constituting consciousness. Meditation and the phenomenological method of reflection reveal an aspect of consciousness that does not appear to be individual, but seems to be cosmic instead. We call that aspect of consciousness transcendental and it has as much reality as any other aspect of consciousness. Our evidence for cosmic consciousness is the same as for the individual consciousness: we experience it (or it is "there" to be experienced). We are urged to enter the transcendental realm of thinking as a response to the phenomenon of death. When we enter that realm our world design shifts. We then organize our world view around the experience of universality and eternity rather than around the experience of individuality and death. In terms of pure logic and in terms of the structure of appearances, both world views are equally valid: they are a consistent organization of the data of experience. Religion, myth, and philosophy have been the social expressions throughout history of the importance of this reorganization of experience. When we thus restructure our experience, enormous changes take place. And it is under these radical circumstances that eternity and immortality become meaningful concepts.

We all know what happens when we view immortality from the aspect of the finite, individual, and consensual consciousness: it becomes a meaningless idea, pure speculation, or superstition. Let us now explore what happens to the concept of death when we view existence from the aspect of eternity.

In discussing the creation of an authentic individual we developed the metaphor or myth of the "invention" of death. If we start with the premise, discovered in meditation, that our subjective consciousness feels as if it were cosmic, then it seems as if we invent death so that by reflecting on it we can realize its illusory nature. Death is like an enzyme or a catalyst; it drops out of the picture after it has done its job and is no longer needed. Death becomes an agent of eternity.

This metaphor is worth some reflection. Should we invent or postulate death—and invent it so thoroughly that we forget we invented it and believe instead that it has always existed, that it is part of the nature of things—for the single purpose of overcoming it? Should we invent death to motivate us to meditation and philosophy, which then lead to the sense of eternity? Is the experience of eternity unattainable without the illusion of death? Death is a reality so fierce that the only even remote hope we have of overcoming it is tied to a life fully devoted to the destruction of death—through medicine, or through philosophy and religion. Is it worthwhile to believe in death—not only in thought but also in flesh and blood—so that, when we overcome it, its conquest will be that much sweeter and more convincing? Perhaps it is true that the sense of eternity—with its rich implications—can be achieved only in a life devoted to overcoming death, and in recognizing death to be consciousness in its state of self-deception. The assumption behind the search for immortality is that the experience of deathlessness, which is also the experience of egolessness, is life's highest value and that no sacrifice is too great to help us totally integrate this insight.

Why have we "invented" death? We have done so in order to truly understand and appreciate the eternity of consciousness. We have invented death—we have challenged our nature (which is to strive to live) by inventing death, so that we can, in the act of philosophically overcoming death, be reminded of the eternity of our consciousness. We have placed death before us as a reminder of what we really are. In the process of overcoming that obstacle, of fighting death, we will discover our true nature. That is the myth in whose terms we must answer the question of why we have "invented" death.

Eternal Consciousness

Let us therefore explore the possibility that there may be an indestructible, eternal consciousness, and that the famous Sanskrit saying, *tat twam asi* (I am indestructible, eternal consciousness) is true. In fact, from the point of view of a transcendental philosophy of pure consciousness, this question of the eternity of consciousness may be the only question worth asking.

The first approach to the question of immortality is experiential and phenomenological, rather than purely logical and analytic. The second is based on an analysis of theological arguments.

THE EXPERIENTIAL APPROACH

I think it is a grievous error to approach the question of immortality exclusively by searching for arguments and proofs. On the contrary, the approach to understanding immortality must include evocative material and not be exclusively demonstrative or deductive. That is a natural consequence of the phenomenological method, which, being a radical empiricism, argues that the only evidence that we are capable of giving for the indestructibility of the conscious center is what is disclosed to us in immediate experience. And that is what our present analysis purports to do. The arguments for immortality begin with Plato's view in the *Phaedo* that the indestructibility of the soul follows from the unitarian nature of the soul, and such reasoning continues throughout the history of philosophy. If taken literally these arguments are irrelevant in the empirical context of existential phenomenology, which is really an expanded scientific methodology. It is the experience—the sensitive description of direct observation—that counts in establishing the reality of immortality.

At best, the arguments for the immortality of the soul developed by philosophers and theologians serve as metaphors to remind us of certain structures in consciousness that can be observed directly. Essential to these structures is the foundation of consciousness that is called the Eternal Now. One warning is in order. When we talk about experience justifying belief in immortality the implication might be that there exist special, unique kinds of experiences—given to a few select souls and at a privileged time as a divine afflatus. I deny that. "Immortality" is a word that describes, evokes, or points to a "visible" and identifiable aspect of *all* experience—present and accessible at all times. The role of the existential-phenomenological philosopher is to describe the *general* traits of *all* experience and to isolate those characteristics that are of special relevance to help us manage the problem of giving or finding life's meaning. In this way a phenomenology of immortality is on the solid ground of facts.

What are facts? Facts are experiences or descriptions of experiences. Unless we can actually experience the eternity of consciousness we are not really achieving anything worthwhile in seeking an answer to death. We must discover what portion of our awareness now *is* this eternal consciousness.

The reason for emphasizing experience is obvious: Suppose that through complex logical calculations we could prove that there exists an immortal soul. These calculations, in themselves, will do nothing for you; they will not change your life. They will not give meaning, change your perceptions, nor will they bring you joy and true peace. They will not make you any happier, unhappier, any more alive, any more dead than you may be now. They will not change your life any more than my proving a mathematical or geometric theorem would transform your life from despair to euphoria, from anguish to peace of mind. Logical proofs are not related directly to questions of living and meaning. Approaching the question of discovering the Eternal Now as an aspect of our experience through argumentation will be fruitless— unless we view the resulting proofs not as solutions to puzzles but as metaphors for the structure of consciousness. Deductive proofs, if they have a role, must be seen in the same light as stories, fables, myths, and fairy tales: metaphors for deeper philosphical truth.

The proofs or arguments for the existence of God have, in my opinion, the same function: *they are logical metaphors* for important structures in experience. They are metaphors drawn from our conceptual life, rather than from our bodily, emotional, or worldly life.

Our task may be of such great proportions that perhaps we should be afraid to go on. Our search for the indestructibility of consciousness, the eternity of consciousness, is to be one fruit and *raison d'être* of the development of an existential-phenomenological personality theory. It is not enough to *demonstrate* to you that consciousness is eternal; you must experience it. That is like telling you that unless you can feel your immortality at this moment, our task will have failed. And it is frightening to think in this fashion. It is as if we were on a life raft adrift in the ocean and someone said to you, "I promise you we can on this spot build an island, with a great castle surrounded with fructifying beauty, where we can be saved and live happily." That is a risky statement.

We can develop some images to help you experience that part of being, that part of your field or the field of consciousness which manifests itself to us as being eternal. One expression which I believe has the power to evoke, bring out, and focus on the Eternal Now is the concept—introduced before but analyzed here in detail—of the *solitary* and *silent center.*

The Solitary and Silent Center

The image of a solitary and silent center is certainly not new. It is as old as humanity. It is the silence of the mind, the prerequisite of meditation.

Let us dwell on this image. Let us stop the activity of our consciousness, which is really not the activity of consciousness itself but of the objects *of* our consciousness, the objects that are *given to* our consciousness. Let us think of a psychedelic movie, a sequence of dizzying lights and colors. Let the film stop, and then gradually disappear like leaves that have fallen into dark waters. Let us stop all the chatter and commotion; the movements of the objects in our minds—the agitation. Then the silent, solitary center emerges as a perfectly real and meaningful expression. It is a term to which corresponds an ever-present locus of experience. Indeed, it is not an experience to which we can *point,* because it is the silent center itself that says, "*stop* the pointing, *stop* all the chatter." We cannot point to it because it is the silent center itself that *does* the pointing. Can you turn off all the content of the consciousness? Can you turn off all the movement, the constant flow, the constant pictures, the images? If you can, the silent center will be given the chance to appear clearly in its purity.

We live in a society that believes in super-saturation, which directly opposes the idea of allowing our perception of the silent center. Our society worships the noisy periphery that is an escape from the solitary, silent center. Saturation and activity, especially when it is aimless and compulsive, tries to fill the emptiness of the silent center; the attempt is to choke and kill the center. The center, which is imperishable, is rescued by the discovery that the killer is really the victim. I still remember the first time I picked up one of my sons at a junior high school dance. I found no way to escape the unbelievable noise of the music. I shut my ears and was shattered by the vibrations in my bones! I remember shouting at the top of my voice but I did not hear or feel a thing. I thought I had completely lost my ability to speak.

Is there any more effective way of squelching the silent center? Alcohol, drugs, compulsive work, compulsive play are but escapist devices we use in trying desperately to run away from this core. Some contemporary art is so busy with color, line, and detail that it produces nausea; we are forced to concentrate on all the dots and movements, lines and color contrasts, and the dizzying and endless details. Our manic culture does not leave us alone; we are being brainwashed; the external world is foisted upon the silent center.

This is a violation of the integrity of the ego.

The Paradox of Self-Referential Statements

Let us now, in our continuing effort to approach the issue of immortality experientially, attempt to make sense of its opposite—namely, the notion of the death of the silent center (called also the transcendental ego); i.e., of the nonexistence or the non-being of the transcendental ego. I hope to show that the concept of the center's non-being is without any meaning. But more of that later.

To understand what could possibly be meant by the death of the transcendental ego we must first explore the philosophic question of self-reference. Any statement about the center (or the transcendental ego) is of course also made by that same center. This statement is then self-referential, and it presents unique logical problems. The search for the meaning of self-referential statements, including those about the transcendental ego, immediately involves incessant and irresolvable conundrums. If we gain some insight into the paradox of self-reference we will also understand the intrinsic nature of the transcendental ego, the ego that is always a subject and can never become an object, and with it we can, through philosophy, develop a "sense of immortality."

Self-referential statements (or systems) are sentences that refer to events or statements, but also, by definition, to themselves. And if a statement applies to itself, then a paradox is engendered. Examples of self-referential statements are "We can know nothing" or "All statements are false." To the extent that the latter statement applies also to itself, it is false, because we claim all statements are false. And if the statement is false then it is not true that all statements are false—in which case it is possible for the statement to be true, and if it is, then all statements are indeed false. There is no end to this circularity.

This point was expressed in an ancient Greek paradox, in which a Cretan says, "All Cretans are liars." He is a Cretan, too, of course, so that if his statement is true, it is, by definition, a lie. Generalizing, we see here the essence of this paradoxical situation: If the statement is true, it is false.

Such a contradictory situation occurs in several places in the study of logic. Self-referential statements (or systems)—those that include themselves in their meaning or their reference—are paradoxical and contradictory.

Explanation

Now we must raise the fundamental question, "What is the meaning of the fact that self-reference leads to contradiction and even meaninglessness?" One popular theory holds that this paradox is a purely linguistic phenomenon, a characteristic of language with no implications for our world views. My position is emphatically different. From my commitment to the phenomenological method in philosophy, which argues that philosophy is the sensitive description of not usually focused aspects of experience, I hold that paradoxes and myths, as well as a great deal of metaphysics, are linguistic expressions which evoke these philosophically important aspects of experience. In other words, the paradox of self-reference is a reflection in language of an extraordinarily important aspect of experience: It is inherently impossible for experience to reflect upon itself, for the ego to perceive itself, for consciousness to study itself. Although these tasks may be impossible, they are nevertheless the most crucial of all. They disclose to us the structure of consciousness and they give us clues to the meaning of immortality. Furthermore, the study of ourselves—or of experience in the mode of self-reference—is the primary task of philosophy. Thus, self-reference is a linguistic reflection of the experiential fact that whenever you try to make the subject you are into an object of study, you get into insurmountable difficulties. And yet this "reduction" (stepping back) is precisely what a philosophy of subjectivity—such as existentialism and phenomenology—is designed to do.

Theory of Types

To get around this difficulty, but only from a purely formal and linguistic point of view, Bertrand Russell developed what he called the *theory of types,* which says, roughly, that we must distinguish levels of language. He distinguishes "languages" from "meta-languages." For example, a book on English grammar is *about* the English language, and therefore it is not—logically speaking—written *in* the English language. The language *of* the book on grammar is not the language *about* which the book discourses; we must talk about two different languages: the language that we speak—the object language—and the language used to talk *about* this object language. We must not confuse these levels of discourse, because if we do, we get into paradoxes.

Russell's theory of types has, for an empirical philosophy such as existentialism, a fatal flaw: He legislates values or critieria for the exploration of the self-referential dimension of experience. Because he artificially distorts language to avoid self-reference, he makes it illicit to explore subjectivity. He tries to prevent language from focusing on ancient philosophical themes by simply ruling questions like "Who am I?" to be illegal! Thus, the only proper task for philosophy becomes the study of objects, which is usually called the scientific enterprise. The study of man—i.e., the study of the nature of consciousness and of subjectivity—originally the primary task of philosophic inspiration— is now to be abandoned altogether. The existential-phenomenological exploration of subjectivity takes a firm stand against such dangerous and nefarious dehumanization.

In sum, what Russell is really saying is that we must not philosophize about the child with separation anxiety. His views forbid delving into the transcendental realm; and with that prohibition, the uses of philosophy have died.

It is not important to say that self-reference is logically impossible. The real issue is that philosophy's central question is that of self-reference. Philosophy was born in order to ask the questions of self-reference. Philosophy was born when human beings decided they were going to ask questions about themselves. Philosophy is a passion about this issue. Man discovered that self-reference was a great mystery, a great miracle, and religion was born at this time—with the discovery that we must ask self-referential questions.

I define philosophy as the passion for asking the question of self-reference. The question introduces us to the mystery of the transcendental ego. And the question, "Can we conceive of the non-being of the transcendental ego?" is the philosophical and experiential approach to the question of immortality.

NON-BEING

We now have in our possession a reasonably complete philosophic image of the structure, nature, or being of consciousness, as the field-of-consciousness theory of the person. We can, therefore, bring the issue of immortality or of the eternity of consciousness to a head. We can do this simply, and emphatically, by exploring whether there can be *any meaning whatever*—either now, in the past, or in the future—to the notion or the concept of the non-being, the nonexistence of that inner consciousness, the center, the transcendental ego. Does the disappearance of the inner consciousness make any sense whatever? That is the question. It must be thoroughly worked through—conceptually and experientially—and integrated into life and thought.

No Meaning

It is important that you, the reader, make this discovery for yourself. But let us be careful to understand what we mean by "yourself." As a human being—that is, as a person, an ego, an individual, an identity—you are not that inward consciousness. But as a trans-human being you are that inward consciousness. Now try to think of that inward consciousness—the transcendental ego—as *not* being; as not existing now, or in the past, or in the future. If you are in touch with that attempt, that fantasy, you will discover with simplicity and lucidity that the concept of the non-being of that inward consciousness is a concept without any possible meaning whatever.

This act of reflection may be the most important meditation exercise in a person's life. In fact, we can go so far as to say that it produces a sense of immortality. If we take the phenomenological method seriously and agree with Edmund Husserl and William James that "the real is the experienced," then we can even argue as follows: Immortality is achieved through this insight and the opportunity for touching the eternal core is lost without it. That is the meaning in Christianity of needing belief (faith, dogma) to be saved. The philosophic insight puts you in touch with your immortal core. Without it you drift away into the realm of pure matter or pure objectivity.

The non-being of consciousness—as idea, experience, or phenomenon—is bereft of all significance and of all content. It has no clarity. Even the remotest possibility of the non-being of the ultimate inwardness that *I am* is devoid of all meaning. If we look closely, we see that the non-being of consciousness is not there and that the idea which that phrase is supposed to represent does not really exist. That crucial fact is illuminated by a study of the self-referential nature of consciousness. Non-being is a meaning that applies only to objects. Nothing means nothing in a context. It means something has been removed within certain parameters. The ego as pure consciousness has the same kind of universality as the space within which objects can be and not be. If I should think, incorrectly, that my inner consciousness is an object (i.e., empirical rather than transcendental), then I indeed can fantasize its nonexistence; but if I know that my inner consciousness is a true subjective center, then I cannot fantasize its non-being under any circumstances.

If I am in touch with the flow of my authentic subjectivity, then it becomes clear to me that the whole question of the non-being of that inwardness is in actual fact only an object of that inwardness and manufactured by that inwardness. The meaning of non-being is *created* by that inwardness. In other words, the meaning of non-being is invented by my inwardness, and my inward flow exists before the invention (or constitution) of non-being as a meaningful concept and image. It follows that my inwardness, my ultimate subjective flow, is prior to any of its inventions, including the object we term the non-being of that very same inward conscious flow.

These are esoteric words, but we are dealing with the ultimate zone of self-referentiality, and words break down. In your effort to develop a sense of eternity now, *you must be urged to imagine, not an object being gone, but the subject that observes all objects being gone.* Then you are invited to realize that to think of the non-being of that inwardness is happily a hopeless task. It cannot be done, because thinking about the non-being of anything is an *action* of an *inwardness.* There must, therefore, always be an inwardness. In other words, no one has ever been able to think the thought of mortality as a subjective phenomenon. To state it in even more peremptory terms, we can say that the accurate meaning of the thought "I am mortal" *has never been thought!* Whenever I do think of "my death" I think not of an inward "me" but an externalized and objectified projection, a constituted invention.

When I argue that we cannot conceive of the non-being of our subjectivity, I am not playing word-games to abolish non-being. It is true that this kind of philosophizing gives us a *feeling* of the immortality of the transcendental self. But it is important to note that in the realm of pure consciousness, feeling is the only available evidence. However, we should not call that evidence a feeling; it is rather a phenomenological description of experience in the reflective or reflexive mode. The only kind of evidence there can be about the structure and the existence of pure consciousness is that which is given to immediate experience, that which appears as phenomenon. The feeling of immortality is therefore the proof for immortality, provided, of course, that feeling is thoroughly examined and shown to be self-authenticating—that is, self-evident.

Suppose someone argues, "Just because we can't imagine our own death, it has no 'meaning' for us, doesn't mean it doesn't happen." But that is precisely the case—"it doesn't happen" makes sense if we re-perceive the world from the point of view of transcendental consciousness. If we take transcendental consciousness seriously and if we allow our descriptions of it to lead us where the argument goes, then the idea of death is seen to be an empirical concept only. What must be understood is that immortality means a radical reconception of the world. Within the world as common sense constitutes it for us, there is no room for immortality. But in a world radically reconstructed by a consistent application of phenomenological techniques, immortality is no mystery, for death has no relevance to the transcendental dimension. If it is now argued further, "We can't imagine one billion people, but they exist," then I respond, "We can approximate imagining that many people. We divide them into groups. We diagram them. We can even draw a billion dots on a flat area of ground and actually see them with our very eyes. Specifically, we can make four clearly visible dots on a square millimeter. If we now maintain this density of dots over an area one hundred meters long and twenty-five meters deep, the size of a small athletic field, we have our billion visible dots. No theory even remotely similar applies to the non-being of transcendental consciousness."

Intentionality

I have elsewhere discussed[1] the "comet theory of objects," which is the view that every object has a stream, or tail, connecting it to a subjective consciousness. This is called, in phenomenology, the theory of

---

[1] *Managing Anxiety* (Englewood Cliffs, N.J.: Prentice-Hall, 1974), Chapter 1. See also p. 105 in this text.

the intentionality of consciousness. In terms of this theory of the structure of consciousness it follows that the idea of non-being, the concept, the icon, the fantasy of non-being—which in phenomenology is called an "eidetic" object; that is, a conceptual object—also has attached to it a stream that connects it to a conscious center. The stream goes not only from object to consciousness, but also from consciousness to object. And that stream of consciousness must be there, must exist, for the idea of non-being to be sustained. It thus follows that the non-being of subjective or inward consciousness—that is, of the transcendental ego, or the transcendental flow—is an idea without any meaning whatever.

The problem for philosophy is not, How can we prove that the soul is immortal? but, How can we explain the rather pervasive inauthentic and common sense belief—a belief that cannot even be formulated, much less demonstrated—in the destructibility of our transcendental region? The answer, if there is one, lies in our proclivity for materialism and objectification, our willingness to lose ourselves, so that we can then again find ourselves. But we must assume full personal responsibility for our belief in death, so that our willingness to lose ourselves is at bottom a free choice, a decision for which we are responsible.

One more comment is in order. We can argue that the act of creating non-being is always subsequent to the existence of the inwardness capable of that creative or constitutive act. Consciousness invents non-being just as it invents death in order to understand its own being. Non-being is an invention of being. Non-being is an invention of this inward consciousness. The idea of non-being is an object just like any other object and has no other meaning.

Integration

I take this way of thinking very seriously, unorthodox as it might be for a professional philosopher trained and practicing in the second half of the twentieth century. Furthermore, I recomment that you, the reader, make every effort to integrate these insights into your life. They may provide the best antidote known to anxiety. They can help remove tensions and release primitive unconscious and creative energies, give life meaning, and help restore many of the precious human values lost in our century of alienation.

I also take seriously the seemingly even more outrageous and unorthodox notion that consciousness is *outside space and time.* Spatial and temporal categories also are, in the last analysis, objects—very basic and universal objects, but objects nonetheless—and therefore they do not describe the innermost vestiges of the subjective consciousness. This ultimate consciousness is strictly *atemporal* and *aspatial.* Time and space, like death and non-being, are its invention. The least objectionable descriptive term designating this indestructible and silent center is the Eternal Now.

Let me conclude by saying that with the above statements I have tried to describe the direct experience of the transcendental ego. I have not attempted proof or demonstration. We must recognize, however, that phenomenology shows that the separation between proof, explanation, and description cannot be made in all instances.

18

The Symbolism
of the Proofs
for Immortality

This chapter will argue that the so-called traditional arguments for the existence of God are conceptual fairy tales intended to give us the experience of the deathlessness of our silent and solitary center. They are symbols and myths—but essential ones—that we must receive if we are to acquire the sense of immortality.

ST. ANSELM

Phenomenology and existentialism are certainly not the first philosophies that have discovered that the non-being of ultimate inward consciousness is an impossible—that is, self-contradictory and unimaginable—concept. There are two dramatic episodes, among many, in the history of Western thought in which the discovery of the power of the Eternal Now was made momentously and with extraordinary consequences. In the eleventh century, the Archbishop of Canterbury, known subsequently as St. Anselm, wrote what has come down to us as the famous ontological argument for the existence of God. Let us look at Anselm's own words:

> ST. ANSELM
> *The Ontological Argument*
>
> *And so Lord, do thou, who dost give understanding to faith, give me, so far as thou knowest it to be profitable, to understand that thou art as we believe; and that thou art that which we believe. And, indeed, we believe that thou art a being than which nothing greater can be conceived. Or is there no such nature, since the fool hath said in his heart, there is no God? But, at any rate, this very fool, when he hears of this being of which I speak—a being than which nothing greater can be*

conceived—understands what he hears, and what he understands is in his understanding; although he does not understand it to exist.

For, it is one thing for an object to be in the understanding, and another to understand that the object exists. When a painter first conceives of what he will afterwards perform, he has it in his understanding, but he does not yet understand it to be, because he has not yet performed it. But after he has made the painting, he both has it in his understanding, and he understands that it exists, because he has made it.

Hence, even the fool is convinced that something exists in the understanding, at least, than which nothing greater can be conceived. For, when he hears of this, he understands it. And whatever is understood, exists in the understanding. And assuredly that, than which nothing greater can be conceived, cannot exist in the understanding alone. For, suppose it exists in the understanding alone: then it can be conceived to exist in reality; which is greater.

Therefore, if that, than which nothing greater can be conceived, exists in the understanding alone, the very being, than which nothing greater can be conceived, is one, than which a greater can be conceived. But obviously this is impossible. Hence, there is no doubt that there exists a being, than which nothing greater can be conceived, and it exists both in the understanding and in reality. . . .

And it assuredly exists so truly, that it cannot be conceived not to exist. For, it is possible to conceive of a being which cannot be conceived not to exist, and this is greater than one which can be conceived not to exist. Hence, if that, than which nothing greater can be conceived, can be conceived not to exist, it is not that, than which nothing greater can be conceived. But this is an irreconcilable contradiction. There is, then, so truly a being than which nothing greater can be conceived to exist, that it cannot even be conceived not to exist; and this being thou art, O Lord, our God.

So truly, therefore, dost thou exist, O Lord, my God, that thou canst not be conceived not to exist; and rightly. For if a mind could conceive of a being better than thee, the creature would rise above the Creator; and this is most absurd. And, indeed, whatever else there is, except thee alone, can be conceived not to exist. To thee alone, therefore, it belongs to exist more truly than all other beings, and hence in a higher degree than all others. For, whatever else exists does not exist so truly, and hence in a less degree it belongs to it to exist. Why, then, has the fool said in his heart, there is no God, since it is so evident, to a rational mind, that thou dost exist in the highest degree of all? Why, except that he is dull and a fool?[1]

Analysis

The ontological argument is a prayer intoned by St. Anselm. In my opinion, he experienced God as the flow of the Eternal Now that pervades his inward consciousness. But he experienced that within the metaphoric structure of the Catholic or Christian Church, and not in a

[1] From the *Proslogium*, transl. Sidney Norton Deane (Open Court, 1903), pp. 1-2, 6-9, 149-51, 158-59. Quoted in John A. Mourant, *Readings in the Philosophy of Religion* (New York: Crowell, 1954).

Hindu, Buddhist, Hebrew, or Islamic context. And he worshipped that consciousness, which is simply a way of being meditatively aware or at one with that eternal consciousness. He was saying, in effect, "Now that I understand what that consciousness is, now that I really have direct access to that eternal subjective consciousness that I am or which runs through me, I recognize that you (God) must exist, that your existence is an inner necessity." The nonexistence of this inward consciousness, or for him, the nonexistence of God, was thus inconceivable. It made no sense, because God's existence is also His nature, or His essence. St. Anselm was praying to that consciousness, which is like saying he was aware of the pure consciousness that he is or that he experiences coursing through him.

The restatement of St. Anselm's prayer continues: "I understand now what is meant by self-reference. I understand now what is meant by the ultimate, inward consciousness which goes beyond my humanity; and reflecting on that makes me realize that the existence of that consciousness is *necessary.* I have discovered experientially the incredible truth that something exists by virtue of its own necessity. God's existence follows from His nature, and His essence; i.e., the fact that He must exist." That was St. Anselm's inspired insight. And that is a description of the vision of the pure consciousness or the Eternal Now that is the matrix of our being.

All of a sudden he seems to have realized that the ontological argument is a description, in scholastic jargon—or a metaphor—of this discovery: Once we understand the nature of consciousness, we realize not only that it goes through us, that it is an integral part of whatever we mean by the terms *self* or *ego,* but that above all that *it must exist.* And this insight is, in my opinion, the essence of the ontological argument.

The ontological argument is a description and evocation of that discoverable fact about our conscious or transcendental nature. It avails itself of Aristotelian logic and of argumentation in general to develop a description of an essential aspect of our own personal experience of transcendental consciousness. In so doing, the argument helps us discover and experience for ourselves who and what we really are, have been, and will be. It may well be historically the most notable of all the arguments for the existence of God. With the appearance of that argument in the history of Western thought—perhaps as early as Plato's *Timaeus*—the insight of the "indestructibility of the inward consciousness that I am" struck the Earth like a thunderbolt. Ever since, the ontological argument for the existence of God has been an important part of the intellectual equipment of the Western world; it endures not for its scholastic intricacies or elegant logic but because of its power to help mankind experience the eternity and indestructibility of the Eternal Now.

DESCARTES

This ontological thunderbolt struck a second time in the seventeenth century with Descartes' famous formula, *Cogito, ergo sum*—I think, therefore I am. Descartes chose to question everything and indeed everything could be questioned. He tried to doubt the existence of everything, and indeed the existence of everything could be doubted. But he discovered, like Anselm, that there was one event whose reality was indubitable, that could in no way be doubted: *his inward consciousness.*

Again, here we are dealing not with a logical argument but with a description of that part of experience which is not objective. We are describing the subjective (or transcendental) realm, the region of pure inward consciousness. Descartes discovered the experiential or empirical *fact* that there was no clear and distinct way in which he could doubt or question the act of doubting itself—that is, his own personal act of doubting. *Cogito, ergo sum* is the same statement and has the same meaning as the ontological argument—except that Descartes' word for consciousness is "ego," whereas St. Anselm's was "God." But the referents of these two terms are indistinguishable, because the transcendental ego is the same as God in the language of existential phenomenology and because there is an amorphous continuum between the infinite cosmic stream of being and the finite individualization of the ego (constituted through the invented life-objects we call my birth and my death).

Empirical and Transcendental Ego

The empirical ego is you, the wordly human being. The empirical realm is the world of nature, in whose evolutionary and involutionary stream you participate and out of which through the constitution of the phenomena of your birth and your death you carve out your sense of being an individual body, person, and social entity.

The transcendental ego is God in you, the eternal consciousness as you experience it *in you.* The transcendental realm is the world of the spirit—which in meditation can be experienced as one and continuous with the empty and eternal cosmos of space and time—out of which you carve your sense of the individual subjective ego again through the inventions of your birth and your death. In this way you assume responsibility for being the individual that you are and at the same time you become aware of your possibilities for infinity and eternity.

And these "truths" are true only to the extent that they are understood and experienced. If an individual does not understand and experience these insights, then his being does not participate in this realm. His being is then truly alienated. He is a piece of rock that has detached itself from its rotating planet and is now spinning aimlessly and forever in the cold, vast darkness of empty space.

Because of St. Anselm and Descartes, the history of Western thought has never been the same. They were two volcanic eruptions of a permanent undercurrent of lava that has always existed and always will exist. Phenomenology, the foundation of existentialism, is—like a "Cartesian Meditation"—a rejuvenation and an updating of the philosophy of Descartes.[2]

In sum, the foregoing analysis suggests that you can be in touch with the pure consciousness in you, and that this consciousness can in no way be conceived of as nonexistent. Your next task is to remember that insight and fully integrate it into your life. The consequences—perhaps narrow and pedestrian—nevertheless can be reduced anxiety, greater control over your life, peace of mind, and the personal discovery of meaning and purpose.

CONSCIOUSNESS AS LIGHT

I shall make one more attempt to clarify how the idea of the indestructibility of consciousness follows from the premise that the person is a field. The field theory is a phenomenological description—that is, a careful evocation of the structure of our human experience bereft of as many assumptions and interpretations as possible.[3]

Our consciousness can be compared to a light illuminating the world. It illuminates many objects, including other persons and minds as well as our own body and mind (i.e., intellect and emotions). We call these the empirical or psychological egos, while the light is the

---

[2] See E. Husserl, *Cartesian Meditations*, transl. Dorion Cairns (The Hague: Martinus Nijhoff, 1960).

[3] See also *Managing Anxiety* (Englewood Cliffs, N.J.: Prentice-Hall, 1974), Master Table, Item A1.

transcendental ego or transcendental consciousness. The diagram on this page illustrates the point.

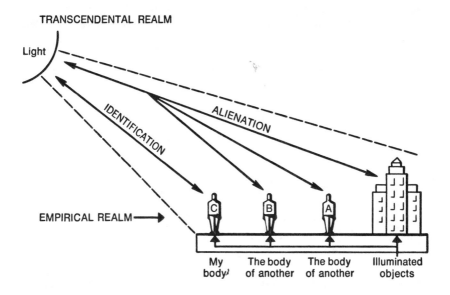

Let us now consider certain facts disclosed by a presuppositionless analysis of our total, not truncated, experience. First, we can observe bodies A and B die. We also observe that the light continues to shine. We have not had the experience of the death of C. We infer, correctly, that C will also die. What happens to the light? If the identification between the light and my body is close, we fear the light will be extinguished with the death of C. If, however, we recognize the *distance* between the light and my body—which is a central tenet of the field theory—then it certainly does not follow that with the death of C the light dims. To argue in this fashion would be to commit a *category mistake*—that is, to argue from the empirical to the transcendental realms, from the referential to the reflexive acts of consciousness. We can argue inductively (that is, generalize from observation) that one event in the empirical realm gives us a clue to another event in the empirical realm. We can also argue that one event in the transcendental realm (although the concept "one event" has confused meaning within the transcendental realm) is evidence for the occurrence of a similar event in the transcendental realm. What we *cannot* do is to confuse realms, types, or categories. We cannot argue from the fact that A dies that the light will go out. If anything, we have evidence that with the death of A *the light remains,* hence, why not argue that with the death of my body the light will also remain?

What does emerge from this analysis is that immortality is an impersonal or a transpersonal experience. In a sense, immortality is the crazy consciousness. The experience of immortality is attained whenever the attachment to the empirical ego (the body) is experienced as loosened. Seeking individual gain and aggrandizement is thus the enemy of immortality. Depersonalization and indifference to human concerns become the hallmark of the consciousness that experiences immortality. These are also the denials of the individual consciousness and, from the latter's point of view, must be seen as schizophrenic conditions.

RESISTANCE—WHY?

When I reach this point with some of my brightest students they sometimes exhibit steely resistance. I rather imagine there may be a bit of that in some of my readers, too. The meaning of that resistance to understanding and perceiving the flow of our consciousness through our humanity is related to a certain confusion about why people become interested in philosophy. That confusion can be cleared up, I believe, through an understanding of two by now familiar phenomenological theses: (1) the distinction between the transcendental and the empirical egos, and (2) the transcendental region as related to the creation of an individual from it.

There is a story of an Indian Brahmin who claimed that he had magical powers but lost them whenever he intended to use them. He said he had these powers, even though they were never shown or materialized—this is not unlike Jesus' refusal to save himself from the cross. In the world of contemporary Western philosophy such a claim typically illustrates the kind of hypothesis which, because it can never by confirmed, is meaningless. It is a hypothesis constructed in such a way that confirming it is by definition impossible. "How do you *know* you have these powers," asks the pragmatically oriented Westerner, "unless you can actually demonstrate them? It is the demonstration that proves the possession. The only meaning of having these powers is that you can show me." This pragmatic or positivisitc analysis holds that the meaning of a sentence is in its consequences, and if the consequences cannot be observed, then there exists no meaning for the sentence.

There Is No Magic

Some persons make a commitment to psychology, philosophy, religion, or theology because they secretly believe they can attain quasi-magical powers through those disciplines. This attitude prevails in some of the fringe fads surrounding contemporary philosophy. Through these insights, perhaps, a person can be superior to his competitor. Maybe he can manipulate someone else to do his bidding. Maybe he can become a demigod who is superior to his fellow men, if he studies with sufficient depth the mysteries of the occult in psychology, philosophy, or religion. Maybe if he prays in a certain way he will succeed in business, or win the election, or win the scholarship, or get ahead in some way that other people cannot. Maybe if he understands these deep issues and goes through transcendental meditation and biofeedback, or psychoanalysis, or whatever, he will gain access to superhuman powers. There are those who will tell you that if you contact the eternal cosmic stream, you can tap it and turn it to your worldly and material advantage.

Thinking such thoughts, some people seek to get in touch with the higher powers and perhaps become a little more like God and a little less like man. *This will never be accomplished.* Although this search may have some theoretical value, it will never work in practice. And if we can understand, as with our Brahmin friend (1) why it might work theoretically, and (2) why it can never work in practice, then we will have understood the relationship between the transcendental and the empirical egos, between the infinite and the finite possibilities for our human existence. Then we will have understood also the meaning of taking responsibility for one's finitude.

A mature person realizes that to make the decision for finitude is also to make the decision to be human rather than divine. And this is not a decision that can be made in both directions at the same time. He will understand how philosophy holds within itself the ultimate disappointment—i.e., the realization that no magical powers will come from it. To understand this fact, it will be necessary for him to give up such a goal. Philosophy may be the last hope in mankind's ancient search for magical powers. But this "hope" amounts to no more than postponing the decision for finitude. When the last hope is given up, the decision for finitude will have been made. No wonder we encounter a resistance at this point!

Clarifying an Ancient Confusion

What is the meaning of the statement that these magical powers, these added strengths, while theoretically consistent with the nature of the transcendental ego, will never be grasped? The very question itself results from a confusion between the transcendental and empirical egos.

The goal of individual supremacy is an empirical, bodily, psychological, individualized, human goal. It is man's ancient goal of power. The isolated empirical ego wants power and survival—disregarding, in a primitive sense, the equivalent needs in others. Democracy and equality are commendable ideals, but the principle of individuation as it operates on the level of biological survival (we individualize ourselves by eating animals which in turn individualize themselves by eating plants, which individualize themselves by competing with other plants for soil, sun, and water, and so forth) can only function with the most grievous compromises and exceptions. Thus, to create individuality by saying yes to oneself always implies the negation and often the destruction of the realm of the *other* in experience.

On the other hand, the transcendental ego is concerned with neither power nor survival. "Power" and "individualization" are meaningless expressions for the transcendental ego. The experience of the cosmic stream of consciousness, of the indestructible, eternal consciousness, is coeval with the understanding of the illusoriness of individual goals, of the artificiality and shallowness of passing particularized, psychological, bodily, or empirical desires.

Give Up the World

As a consequence, we can be in touch with the eternal stream of consciousness only if we have given up all of our individualized goals—including supremacy, power, and even survival. It is only by giving up "this" world that you will gain "the other." It is only by giving up the desire for supremacy that you can be in touch with the Eternal Now and thus, in a metaphoric sense, "be supreme." Should you try to harness the power of the Eternal Now for purposes of individual supremacy, then, at that very moment, you will no longer be in touch with the Eternal Now because you no longer understand what you are doing. You are at that instant identified with the empirical individual that you are, the "illusory" ego.

In actual practice you may find you will never be prepared to give up your identification with the individual ego. You may give it up only in words. You may find that in truth you hope to harness the powers of the Eternal Now for the needs of the narrow, selfish, egocentric desires of an individual ego. And that project will never work, because the only way you can ever be in touch with the Eternal Now, the indestructible consciousness that you are, is to give up the individual now, that with which your Eternal Now identifies itself and through which it loses itself. You must know, however, that with the surrender of your individuality you also give up your worry about dying, because dying is the fear for the individual ego, the individual body, and its limited and isolated existence. Only by giving up the limiting cathexis of, or identification with, the empirical ego can you achieve an understanding of the transpersonal Eternal Now.

Camus

Camus—the atheist and the believer in human finitude—nevertheless expresses beautifully this insight of surrender to the cosmic and of indifference to the human when he has Meursault say, at the end of *The Stranger*, ". . . gazing up at the dark sky spangled with its signs and stars, for the first time, the first, I laid my heart open to the benign indifference of the universe. To feel it so like myself, indeed, so brotherly, made me realize that I'd been happy."[4]

It therefore follows that if you do not have an understanding of these matters, it is because you are holding on to the empirical ego, to its exclusivity, and to its supremacy. You insist on viewing life from the empirical rather than from the transcendental perspective.

If you find yourself fighting what I am saying about your cosmic nature, it is because in order to understand this point you have to give up something that you are not yet ready to give up. In order to achieve the insight about the indestructibility of the Eternal Now that *you are*, you must first give up the individual commitment to the things that you have associated with your name, with your individual and empirical ego: Give up your money, your ambition, your individuality, give up your name. Such surrender is understandably difficult.

[4] Albert Camus, *The Stranger*, transl. Stuart Gilbert (New York: Vintage Books, 1959), p. 154.

THE MONASTIC VOWS

To help, there exist three universal vows for the monastic, ascetic life. These are celibacy, obedience, and poverty. These decisions and commitments are three practical ways to practice severing your hardened and clutching identification with the empirical ego. Remember that in terms of our present theory, to be human means, *first,* to identify the universal and cosmic transcendental ego (or the Eternal Now) which you are with a small object within that cosmos, your bodily and psychological existence (your empirical ego). And it means, secondly, to *forget* or repress that this identification has taken place. To be human, then, is to choose self-deception about the Eternal Now.

Let us analyze the vows individually. First, there is poverty. In our culture—in which money is a primary vehicle of self-identification through which we gain power and satisfy our need for self-assertion, and from which value and meaning are calculated in terms of bank accounts, interest rates, and capital gains—the idea of a monastic vow of poverty encounters much resistance. We have been taught that poverty can only be a problem, never a solution. But poverty can be a virtue, because giving up the dollar could lead to a philosophical understanding of our human nature.

The second vow is to give up sex, which our culture makes even more difficult. Giving up sex is giving up manhood and womanhood, self-assertion and individuality; it is to tamper with our biology. The transcendental ego and the Eternal Now are not sexually seductive concepts. They are not saleable ideas. Asceticism is not difficult in a fully liberated non-Puritanical society; but in a Puritanical society, transcending sex is difficult. A Puritanical society, which is a repressed society, finds in sex its ultimate meaning. Pornography can exist only in a Puritanical society, and so can romanticism, because the miracle of sex lies in its mystery.

A liberated society, one that perceives sex to be as natural as any other bodily function, such as eating and defecating, understands that the truth about human consciousness is not tied to sex. Therefore, asceticism with regard to sex can be a natural consequence of understanding the Eternal Now. Furthermore, sex is the act of an individual. It occurs only after the implementation of the principle of individuation. It is an *individual* act which perpetuates the *individual* species. Giving up sex contributes to the denial of your individuality, as does poverty.

The final monastic vow is obedience. Our contemporary culture makes it difficult for us to be obedient. First-time visitors to the United States are impressed by the arrogant independence of the average American. However, it soon becomes apparent that this arrogance is a manifestation of the sense of individuality exhibited by the "typical" American. Most foreigners are amazed at the contempt many Americans feel for authority. But they soon discover that this attitude is the best-known antidote for fascism.

The vow of obedience is the elimination of self-assertion. Self-assertion is an act of individualization and thus denies the impersonality and detachment of both the sense of transcendental consciousness and of the extra-spatio-temporal Eternal Now. Practice in obedience is a meditative exercise that places the individual in touch with his eternal roots.

These three monastic vows—however difficult to undertake—provide a traditional way in both the Eastern and the Western cultures to contact the Eternal Now.

Now, having dealt with perhaps the most esoteric and difficult concepts in this book, the pendulum can swing back to the experiential.

The following chapter suggests some guided daydreams and related fantasies to help achieve the actual experience of the deathlessness of consciousness.

19

Immortality Exercises

THE STRUCTURE OF THE EXPERIENCE
OF IMMORTALITY

The experience of immortality (or intimations of it) can be achieved by de-constituting (or de-organizing) the invention, creation, or consti- tution of the ego or of the sense of individuality. We must first re- experience the archetypal decision to be an individual—as it is dis- cussed in this book—and then turn time around and reverse this pro- cess. Rather than focusing on individuality, we must encourage and develop the experience of "oneness-with," of cosmic unity. That expe- rience of universality as opposed to individuality is to be achieved in each one of the three primary areas of the field of consciousness: *ego, cogito*, and *cogitata*—the source, the stream, and its object.

We have discussed how to achieve universality from the point of view of the ego, the source, the transcendental region: that is the ac- tivity of asceticism and withdrawal. It is also true that the principal schism in the field of consciousness is between the ego (in this case the transcendental ego) and the world. Therefore, if we wish to expe- rience immortality in our posture of world involvement, of participa- tion in the flow of nature, then we must cultivate our potential for unity with (a) the *process* of living and (b) the *body* and its at-homeness in its environment (which is nature). We must learn to experience the body, its processes, and its comfortable integration in the environment as a life of its own. This is the experience of unity with nature, of abandon to the body, its feelings and needs. It is the phenomenon of commitment. It is the opposite experience of ascetic withdrawal. However, in order to achieve this sense of unity, not with pure ego-consciousness, but with nature, we must practice perceiving ourselves, not as *individual* processes (intentions) and bodies (cogitata), but as *one* whole and total observed ecological system. In this case we merge not with universal or cosmic *consciousness*, as does the ascetic, but with universal and cosmic *nature*. Our will becomes the will of evolutionary processes and natural forces. We have given up physical (or empirical) individuation. Going to sleep is a prelude to that experience of abandonment to nature.[1] We can thus search for immortality either by ascetically withdrawing into the inner realm of our pure conscious center or by aesthetically and sensuously abandoning ourselves to total identification and involvement with the flow of nature.

By religiously pursuing the following didactic exercises—which emphasize the ascetic solution to death—we can have, as individuals, premonitions and adumbrations of the experience of immortality. The key dynamism bringing about this realization is relinquishing the sense of being an individual, undoing or reversing the archetypal decision to be an individual.

A GUIDED DAYDREAM

At the beginning of this book we talked about a positive approach to death. I can think of no more appropriate way to bring to an end a book about the existential approach to death than by asking the reader to participate in a series of what I call immortality exercises. These can put you in touch with the ascetic, pure, transparent, inward, silent, solitary, and flowing center of consciousness that you are. They can also put you in touch with that deep region of inner peace which is the Eternal Now. In this sense you can at this moment experience the meaning of immortality, and, even beyond that, the fact that the consciousness that courses through you is indeed timeless and indestructible.

Such ascetic withdrawal is not life's *summum bonum*. It is one of at least two fundamental possibilities for human existence. We may opt for mystical asceticism or for its opposite, individual involvement. If we choose the former, these exercises can give us the experience of pure transcendental consciousness. If we choose the latter, they can open for us the ground from which and out of which arises the deci-

---

[1] The experiences of *immortality* and *grounding* are closely related.

sion to be an individual, and out of which emerges the resoluteness of taking responsibility for being ourselves.

The first exercise is a guided daydream, a fantasy. I want you to draw a mental picture of yourself as a dying patient in a hospital. Allow me to suggest the fantasy to you.

> You are lying in pain in a hospital, dying, having been in agony and confined to this hospital bed for a long time. You know that this is the end, and you feel very much abandoned. Friends do not visit you any more; they no longer consider you part of themselves. In fact, they seem to wish that you'd get it over with and die. Now meditate on your pain, so that gradually you change from being your pain to watching it as if it were not part of you. As you gain this sense of detachment, the moments of pain will become less painful, and the trancelike flickers of painlessness become episodes of relief and of peace—maybe even of joy. You are so used to your pain that it seems strange not to be in pain; painlessness is like a foreign land. Your pain was your constant companion, your guide in redesigning the world for you, your reminder of your existence. But now this pain has become a distant event.
>
> The nurses now respond only rarely to your calls and the doctors appear to have lost interest in you; you are, after all, proving to them their incompetence by dying. And you are losing interest in communicating with them. You are beginning to feel comatose, and you are thereby becoming reconciled to the fact that you are now dying, something that you know without ever being told. In this condition you are immensely peaceful, although completely indifferent. And that is because you are withdrawn from the world.

Receding

I will now describe to you what your thoughts will be when you are about to die.

> Those things and events which we call human are beginning to recede. They are now becoming smaller; you can barely perceive them in the distance. And those receding worldly objects include your very own body—you now see your body "over there," in that distance. The distance makes even your body very small. Everything that is individual, that is human, that is you, that is part of the social world in which we live, all that has now receded into this distance. And you now feel more like a god in outer space observing life than a human being participating in the affairs of this world. At that moment you are in touch with the pure and universal consciousness. Consciousness no longer cares about these worldly things, even the fact that it is indestructible. You feel an infinite peace; and it feels natural. Whereas to the ex-person whom your consciousness is now abandoning this peace would have been a value, you, in your holy indifference, now no longer care.
>
> You are that comatose patient, abandoned in a far room of the hospital; and you can catalog some of the things that are receding into the distance, that to you are no longer goals, no longer truths, no longer realities, but only meaningless baubles making sense only in an illusory age and a mythical world that you no longer

recognize as real. One of these objects is pain. Pain once was a terrible problem but now it does not seem that way at all; the image that pain is terrible has receded.

Death itself is another receding object. There was a time when you believed that dying was the worst thing in this world. That fear makes no sense anymore. You fail to understand how you could ever have thought that way. Death to you is now the gentle comforter. Death seems even a greater peace than what you are feeling right now. And while you now feel only partially "in the hands of the Lord," when you will be truly dead you think that you will be "totally in the hands of the Lord." You can no longer understand how you ever felt death to be bad; death is the natural conclusion of a life that is mostly unsatisfactory and far too complicated. Despair does not exist any more. Despair is what people talk about as being over there in the distance. They are the desperate ones. To you anxiety and bitterness have no real meaning anymore; they belong to a past age; they are as unreal to you now as you lie dying as Adolf Hitler and World War II are unreal to today's children; they form no part of their real experience.

Hope, success, sex, education, reputation, fame—all those things, what are they? They are bagatelles that dolls talk about in doll houses. They are receding values which you no longer wish to appropriate as your own. At one time, perhaps, you were attached to them, but you no longer are excited about that identification. All of these values are receding into a meaningless distance; they have ceased to be either truths or realities.

Reconciliation

And now you discover, with this fantasy, that you are reconciled with death, that you in fact welcome it, and that you are at peace. All of these trinkets that were important to you at one time are what do make you human, but they do that by limiting you. Identification with those objects, grasping them passionately, holding on to them and identifying with them as if they were the truths—these experiences limit you; they are the key to your individuality and separateness. Now you experience yourself as universal. And you have no reason to doubt the truth of your experience—its accuracy, validity, and reality. You are now at peace; and you now know the meaning of the Divine. You now have a sense of the eternity of pure consciousness.

And death, at this moment, is also unreal. This is it. All you are is aware. You will totally lose interest in this world, and drift away into pure consciousness, dehumanized, totally beyond humanity; and you will have no interest in returning to the sense of being an individual.

You are now experiencing the reverse of the history of creation. As you lie dying, the history of the creation of the world is being shown to you in a film played backwards. Let me describe to you the history of creation, the reverse of your film: There exists—as you are now—a completely vacuous, empty consciousness. That totally transparent, purposeless, contentless consciousness gradually creates—condenses—a cluster of fog within itself, gradually creates a being. That fog slowly grows into a hard, atomic core. And as that being becomes more and more perceptible, the identification of consciousness with that core becomes more and more pronounced. An alienated individual core is, through consciousness' power of constitution, carved out of the plenitude of Being. Suddenly you find yourself an individualized human be-

ing on the planet Earth, totally absorbed in playing the game of life, and ignoring any knowledge you may have had of how this came about. Such is now the reversal of the process of dying. On the deathbed this process goes back and forth, like breathing in and breathing out, inhaling and exhaling.

That is my image of a person reconciled with death. Now, which side is up and which is down? Who has the correct perspective on existence? The dying patient? Or the living survivor? Maybe we can keep turning the world around, spinning it, and when we breathe out the comatose patient's side is up and when we breathe in, the young baby's view, born with all life ahead of him, is up. Such is the idea that life is a cyclical process between the subjective, conscious, and the objective, worldly poles that make up the existence of human beings. This situation is reminiscent of the story of the man who dreams he is a butterfly and who, upon awakening, asks himself whether he is a man dreaming that he is a butterfly or a butterfly dreaming that it is a man.

A MEDITATION EXERCISE FOR DISTANCE

This meditation exercise is more difficult than the previous one: it requires practice, guidance, and patience. First, let your mind wander—an attitude that is the key to many meditation exercises. Cease exerting control over your ideas and your images; let them appear by themselves. Your meditation will resemble a dream: images appear of their own accord. Relinquish your control over these images. Detach yourself from them. Put yourself in a passive rather than an active mood. Allow mental events to happen; do not force them. Such efforts will help you detach yourself (that is to say, your consciousness) from the objects of your consciousness; they will loosen your identification with the objects of your consciousness and thereby put you in touch with the observer aspect of you rather than the you who is the agent. That is a difficult task. We, in our individualistic West, are very agent-oriented; we insist on being active and are focused on willpower. But you should now turn your back to that and appreciate the wisdom of being passive. Do not resist this effort; it is not humiliating to be passive. To reject passivity is to resist transcendental consciousness. You must now become an observer of even your will itself.

The consciousness that you touch in this kind of an exercise may be depersonalized, but it is also experienced to be eternal.

A Tree

Let us, in this meditation exercise, use the analogy of the tree and the soil. The tree is your consciousness and the soil represents the world. To exist is for the roots to penetrate and grab the soil. But now, in your fantasy, let the soil dissolve. Or better yet, gingerly remove the tree with its roots from the soil, shaking off the dirt as you do it. Your consciousness is the bare-rooted tree. The world is the soil. They are now separated and you can observe and study the tree and its roots in isolation. Now observe your newly acquired distance from all the world's objects. Actually sense, savor, experience that distance. Such is the experience of recession. Notice how the objects, when you are thus passive, come and go; how they may diminish in size, in importance. Note that the image of moving away from earth and into outer space is an apt one.

Because to observe and clearly experience the distance between you and your objects is crucial to this meditation exercise, it is useful to proceed in an orderly sequence, to establish a hierarchy of objects. Begin by experiencing yourself as remote from objects that would normally be distant. Increase their remoteness from you—physical distance as well as emotional detachment. Then gradually turn to objects that normally would be very close, such as significant persons and intimate friends and relatives, your cherished possessions, your body— outer limbs as well as inner organs—and finally your ideas, your hopes, and your emotions. Realize that you are not them; recognize that your consciousness exists apart.

Specifically, try to experience the distance of your silent, solitary center from your concepts and ideas, precisely those phenomena which traditionally are thought to be closer to your center than physical objects. But this common belief is not necessarily true. Focus on an idea or a concept and try to be conscious, not of the concept that is allegedly close to you, but on the *distance* that exists from you to that concept. Let that concept recede into the distance and keep your inner eye on the distance.

Now proceed likewise with a feeling, especially an emotion as close and sticky as anxiety or love, and perceive that feeling now as also distant from your silent and solitary center. You feel now as if you were moving out of your body. You no longer feel that you *are* your body but you now clearly experience the fact that you *have* a body, that the center which you are exists at a distance even from your own body.

The Body

Now focus on that body, especially the inner organs, and try to experience not your body but the *distance* between you and your body. You now are in an altered state of consciousness in which you perceive your body, observe your body, and as an observer you have become distant from your body. And now you have taken what may well be your most crucial step: You experience your body not as you but as distant, even separate, from you. If you are able to experience the actual distance from your center to your body then you are on the way to really knowing, understanding, and experiencing your pure consciousness.

We must accustom ourselves to perceive the world (our bodies in particular) always in this fashion and to integrate this ancient wisdom into our total life project. It is important to get used to living these insights, because such integration means that the person lives all of the possibilities of a field-of-consciousness theory of Being.

You are now ready to get even closer to the center. Experience your heartbeats.[2] Experience them as a magnificent symbol of life itself, as something you observe rather than as something you are. It is not *your* heartbeat but *a* heartbeat that the inner center is now observing. And the anxiety of dying will return at this point. It is as if you were saying, "Maybe if I tempt my transcendental ego at this point and really allow myself to experience my heartbeats as something that occurs externally to me, then, because I have lost the control that comes with identification, perhaps the heartbeats will stop! And I am afraid!" As long as you care you are not detached. When you cease to care then you are really detached and you experience your immortality fully. That is a real experience, and it must be recognized as self-authenticating. Many people cannot confront the anxiety of death and should not go beyond that point in this immortality exercise.

A SENSE OF ETERNITY

You can even go beyond the detachment from the empirical ego. The last physical reality, or object, that you should focus on is your

---

[2] Many people become anxious when they experience their pulse. The reason for that anxiety is, I think, the ambiguity about control. Heartbeats equal life. Do I control the heartbeats? If not, then I do not control life. Do I in fact control them? Then why do I irresponsibly allow that control to elude me?

breathing; we have discussed that already in Chapter 13. You can learn to breathe not as if *you* were doing the breathing but as if it were being done outside you, automatically, by someone other than your silent and solitary center. Observe your breathing: *you* are not taking air into yourself; air is being taken into a pair of lungs which are no longer you. And at that moment you may be as close as you can ever be to the direct experience of your Eternal Now, to sensing the pure consciousness that runs through you and that you are. You will also discover that all these phenomena, concepts, feelings, thoughts, sensations, heartbeats, and breathing from which you have now distanced yourself—the complex which in a phenomenological philosophy we call "the Other"—all have a life of their own. They live and act in their own way without your control.

You are now indeed an eternal observer of what happens in this world. You are now in touch with your pure, eternal, indestructible, and unchanging consciousness. You now have a sense of eternity; and at this moment you are the Eternal Now. You are in touch with that one part of ultimate reality we usually ignore. You no longer feel strictly limited and human; you have now transcended the experience of being human. You cannot experience the Eternal Now in human terms nor identify yourself at this moment with being human, because you have now receded from anything finite, including the human.

SELF RE-CREATION

The last step of this exercise is to go back from your condition of detached universality to the attached and committed state of being a finite individual. You cannot be left in this transpersonal state. Now you are in a meditative mood; you are almost totally removed from the objects of this world. Now go back; allow yourself slowly to return to this world. Allow yourself to be once more "incarnated"—go through the steps of re-creating yourself. You will reorganize your world the way it was for you before you experienced the Eternal Now. Although you will return, you will never be the same again, because you will always remember the experience of infinite peace that you found. And that peace will be translated into everyday life and manifest itself there as compassion, love, and peace of mind.

He who has never been in this eternal space may say, "It is important to be compassionate because that is the best policy." But the person who has come back from this profound meditative experience will be lovingly compassionate simply because it is normal and natural; he will be but a reflection of the transcendental nature of the conscious-ness-man-world field.

When you have come back, re-created your humanity and assumed new responsibility for it, you will remember the reality of your transcendental experience. You did not have a dream; nor were you hallucinating. You were truly in touch with one part of real existence that our culture has denied, repressed, and expelled from consciousness. Because you were in touch with that ultimate reality, you come back with courage and strength. You will no longer succumb to fear; you have even conquered the fear of death. Courage is the easy and natural path of life.

And because the eternity of the experience will be remembered, the peace and the timelessness of it will translate themselves in your life into a sense of confidence, relaxation, and security. Your life can now be lived with simple grace. Gone is the hurry, the anguish, the despair, the panic; there is no further need to protect yourself against anxiety. Gone will be compulsive behavior and obsessive ideas.

We have now come full circle. The cancer patient with whom we started may not have understood—in a conscious and literal sense—the material we have been discussing. Nevertheless, we have a right to assume that the insights developed in this book, which amount to a compressed, modernized, and organized restatement of ancient wisdom, were available to her as part of the inheritance of the race, an aspect of the collective unconscious given to her at birth.

If I have any hope for this book at all, if it has had worth and meaning for you, it is that you, now that you have finished reading it, are prepared to find your answer to death—and in so doing, also discover a meaning to your life.

REMEMBER

1. We can perceive death as something that is invented to facilitate the experience of immortality (Chapter 17).
2. The word "immortality" refers to a universally accessible aspect of all experience (Chapter 17).
3. Arguments for immortality are metaphors to describe crucial structures in subjective consciousness (Chapter 17).
4. The indestructibility of consciousness can be an actual experience (Chapter 17).
5. Self-referential statements are verbal metaphors for the infinite-regress structure of subjective consciousness itself (Chapter 17).

6. Philosophy is a passion for self-reference (Chapter 17).

7. "The nonexistence of the transcendental ego" is an expression that has no meaning (Chapter 17).

8. "Non-being" is always an object to consciousness and never refers to the consciousness of which it is the object (Chapter 17).

9. Arguments for the existence of God are logical metaphors describing the subjective, transcendental region of all experience (Chapter 18).

10. The proof that I exist (Descartes) is a metaphor for the experience of the indestructibility of subjective consciousness (Chapter 18).

11. Consciousness is the light that makes objects appear. We commit a "category mistake" if we infer that the death of an object implies the extinction of the light that shines on it (Chapter 18).

12. Immortality cannot be put in the service of selfish concerns (Chapter 18).

13. The experience of immortality appears when we give up the quest for power (Chapter 18).

14. The experience of immortality can be described as the Eternal Now (Chapter 18).

15. The experience of immortality occurs when we "de-constitute" our sense of individuality (Chapter 19).

16. We can experience immortality either by
    a. Identification with the stream of pure consciousness or by
    b. Identification with the stream of nature (Chapter 19).

Exercises

1. The monastic vows of celibacy, poverty, and obedience are practical suggestions for experiencing the distance of consciousness from its objects (Chapter 18).

2. A fantasy about dying can help you experience your indestructible and timeless core (Chapter 19).

3. A fantasy about "distancing" and "detachment" can approximate the experience of the Eternal Now (Chapter 19).

4. *Observing* rather than *being* your heartbeats and your breathing can give you the experience of the indestructible, pure, subjective consciousness that you are (Chapter 19).

APPENDIXES

The Elderly Person
and the Physician
in our Society

How can philosophy be of assistance in the problem of aging? This issue is obviously related to death; if there is one fact common to all old people other than their ostracism from society, it is that they are more conscious of the reality of death than are younger individuals. Their failing bodies are constant reminders. And as they become aware of their increasing infirmity they also come in contact with another reality worthy of examination here; the physician, who has a role similar in power to that of the priest of Medieval Europe.

THROUGH THE BODY, NOT THE MIND

A physician, by training, works through the body, not the mind. And there is a good reason why the patient supports this approach. Because dying is difficult to manage within our subjectivity, we expel or project it outside our consciousness. We in effect say, "Death is an issue that I cannot handle within myself; therefore it is a bodily issue that somebody else can handle mechanically." If I convince myself that my problems are physical, then I relinquish direct responsibility for them. It follows that if I can convince myself that dying is a bodily phenomenon, then I also can relinquish responsibility for my death. Dying then becomes something that happens only to my body. There exist "mechanics," who can work on my body; they can comfort me and solve the problem of death for me. I will resist the philosophic insight that dying is my personal problem and that only I alone can die my own death, that I have to manage my own death. I will resist realizing that the burden of dying is on me! Therefore I demand an arrangement that excuses me from worry. Someone else can worry for me and take care of me. And the only way that I can feel my problem of death is being handled by someone else is to think that the problem is purely physical, not manageable in terms of my conscious field.

If you go to an existential therapist he expects that the improvement of your condition is up to you, and that your health is directly proportional to the commitment you are making to your own life and to your own values. But the person who goes to a physician is not told that it is up to him to cure himself; he may be told to lie down and that it will hurt just a little bit and then he will be better.

This analysis is of course vastly oversimplified, but the basic issues have been raised.

THE ROLE OF THE PHYSICIAN

A physician is expected to perform a specific role. To the extent that he fulfills it he is liked by society, and he is disliked to the extent that he may not fulfill it. I do not refer to the physician as an individual, but only to the role that society has created for him. The individual physician is as much subservient to that role as are the rest of us to our roles.

The physician's role is to be the manager of the dying. When we have death problems we go to a physician, because he presumably knows something about the process of dying and how to overcome it or avoid it.

In other words, we expect the physician to help us conquer death; our psychological attitude toward him is colored by this need. We want someone to help us with death and the physician brings that help. And that need is, in itself, the preamble to a relationship that has curative powers. Whe you are threatened by death, you are highly suggestible. Your are likely to believe almost anything told to you. When you are in this state, you can be helped by authority as much as by medicine.

Many doctors are silent, enigmatic, and laconic; they release only a minimum of information. Some patients object to that approach and, on what appear to be good rational grounds, complain, "Why don't you doctors treat me like an adult and share with me a comprehensive analysis of my condition?" There may be, however, a higher reason for that silence, for that sparsity of information. In a sense, the physician's unconscious demands it, the patient's unconscious demands it, and, even more than that, society itself demands such reticence. This distanced and mysterious attitude itself possesses curative powers. If the physician becomes too human, too close, he will lose this power; he will no longer be believable as a manager of death. A primitive man can go to his medicine man, or his shaman, and that can have the same effect on him that going to a physician has on us—as long as we accept the culturally supported belief that he can manage death.

If my physician gives me too many details and too many qualifications and explanations, I will make the dangerous discovery that he is not a magician but rather a human being like me, and that in the last analysis he is no more able to manage death than I am. When I am threatened by death I do not want to be helped by a human being, a person who is just a little more learned in certain areas than I am; I want to have the help of a superhuman savior—as Jung's analysis of archetypes suggests. Most patients therefore conspire with the physician to keep intact the image of the medicine man and the magician. Such projections onto physicians are important because healing is more than medication and treatments. Suggestion is an important tool for effective medicine.

THE SOCIAL PERCEPTION OF THE PHYSICIAN

Why would a person want to become a physician in the first place, given that the task he is expected to perform by society is impossible? Why would someone want to take up this most difficult role of manager of death? We must realize that physicians are part of the culture, and that they can be expected to have the same expectations of themselves that other people have of them. They want to save lives. So they, too, must believe that death can be managed on the physical level alone and that they can really help their patients. In fact, they may need to believe it even more than the ordinary person. One might deduce hypothetically from the very fact of their being physicians that they are more anxious than the average member of the population about death—their own or other people's. If this analysis is correct, then the physician, when he faces a dying patient, confronts a double anxiety: first, the actual, imminent death of his patient, which may produce above-average anxiety in the physician; and second, his own basic helplessness in this situation. The meaning of life for the physician will be defeated with the death of his patient. Death, though inevitable, is proof of the failure of his art. We can infer that it is emotionally and philosophically difficult to be a physician in our society.

The physician, faced with the death of a patient, must think along these lines: "I went into medicine to hope for physical immortality—so that I could prolong life, because I dread death even more than the average person. And now the very thing is happening that I wanted to prevent."

It is my opinion that the meaning of this mostly unconscious relationship of the physician and the patient must be understood, recognized, and ultimately overcome. When it comes to the issue of dying, we cannot expect the physician to do it for us. Ultimately, we must do it ourselves.

If these statements have some meaning and truth, it follows that the physician himself has a particularly difficult time dying. Whom can *he* look up to? Who is going to comfort *him?* Who is going to do the bodily work for *him?* It is cruel of society to expect physicians to be all-knowing, to have magical powers, even though it may give the rest of us some solace. Conferring such powers makes physicians[dying that much more difficult, because it demands a kind of maturity of them which is not asked of other people.

Education for Aging

A THOUGHT ON THE MANAGEMENT
OF DEATH IN THE ELDERLY

Let us discuss now the issues with philosophical relevance that are likely to arise for old people who are confronted with death. Let us assume that you are the leader, the facilitator, or therapist for a group of aged people and you must confront the issue of the philosophical management of their death. I have some suggestions on how philosophy can help.

First, you have to be able to handle the problem yourself. No one can do it for you. The subjective management of the problem of dying or getting older is *your* problem, because you are a human being and because you are a consciousness.

Next, you must be aware of the infinite adjustability of human beings. I believe that a person can find his meaning under almost any circumstances if he makes a decision to so do. It is also my opinion that a human being can adjust himself to any circumstances—*if* he has made the corresponding decision. And one way to help a person make the decision that he can accept death is through the quasi-hypnotic phenomenon of suggestibility. A healer can suggest to his patient that death is acceptable. He can thus desensitize his patient from the anxiety of death. He can make it clear that the thought of death need not be unbearable, and that this consideration applies to both one's own death and the death of others. If the healer speaks with adequate authority he can change the perception of death as ultimate horror and anxiety to something that is perfectly acceptable, normal, and routine.

All these considerations are based on the infinite adaptability and flexibility of man. Philosophically, this kind of approach is a direct out-growth of the existential theory that man is free—free to define his own meanings, free to choose his self-concept and his identity.

UNFINISHED BUSINESS

Another approach to death that you can use both for yourself and as the therapist for a group of elderly people is to see it as an adventure. It can be an experience with several ramifications, one of which is to finish your unfinished business. This notion can have considerable power, value, and meaning. Life is a series of postponements and procrastinations. Some of the business of living is never even thought about. Often we do not recognize what our unfinished business really is. We are even incomplete in our understanding of what *is* our unfinished business!

One of the aspects of the adventuresomeness of the later years of life is that it may then be easier for us to conclude some of our unfinished business.

You might have your group members make a list of their unfinished business in this life. You will find this to be an interesting experience. To some, it may be uncomfortable. But if people force themselves to admit that they do have unfinished business, they are also forcing themselves thereby to come to terms with the question of their meanings. There is power in that approach. A group of elderly people can be helped to actually conclude some of their unfinished business. This may involve getting relatives to visit them, or visiting relatives and friends; it may mean settling some legal affairs, writing letters, reading books, pursuing some long-delayed hobbies, and so forth.

SUICIDE

We have touched upon this subject before, but there is an application here as well. Certainly anyone who is threatened with meaninglessness and pain late in life confronts the thought of suicide, and it should be discussed. As one person said, "I am getting older and older; my teeth are falling out, my hearing is bad, I am developing cataracts in my eyes. My family is leaving me. I have arthritis, and am in constant pain; most of the time I am doped up with medication. The doctors are nice enough to me, but there is little they can do. It is hard for me to get around. I can hardly walk; I hate to look at my body. Why should I suffer through all this? I have lived my life, and it has been a good one. I shall put my affairs in order and then end it all at what seems to me to be the right time."

Suicide can never be directly recommended to anyone, of course, but nevertheless a responsible philosophical analysis of the issue of the management of death in the elderly must certainly include a courageous and open discussion of suicide.

PREPARATION FOR OLD AGE

The following schema of the development of life can be useful in helping older people achieve meaning and dignity in their last years. Several concepts are involved. One is that human existence is the conflict between man and God, between time and eternity, between the individual and the universal, between the particular and the cosmic. This point is discussed earlier in the book. Another is the idea that to exist as an individual is to have made the free and anxious decision to condense the diaphanous cosmic consciousness into a centered and clustered creative-erotic energy core. That concept is also discussed and analyzed in earlier pages.

Life consists of an evolutionary and an involutionary period. These periods should converge, in adulthood and middle age, in a fully developed sense of individuality (see diagram). At the beginning of life, the infant experiences himself to be one with the cosmos. Even though mind and matter may not be differentiated for him, it can be argued that for him being is mostly objective, material; it is *nature* rather than consciousness or spirit. During the evolutionary period the child says "no" to large regions of being, thereby separating an isolated ego. In adulthood, that ego is highly developed (in the case of authentic persons). As the involutionary period sets in, the debilitating body invites the release of the spirit. The end of life is like the beginning, with an abandonment of individuality and the identification with the cosmos. In this case the totality is experienced as consciousness or as spiritual rather than as matter or nature.

Anxiety is minimal or nonexistent at the beginning and the end. When one is merged with the cosmos (no matter whether it is as nature or as consciousness), one is not anxious. But when a person must sustain being an individual, must continuously recreate himself freely out of the nothingness that is his godliness, then the condition of anxiety is the supreme excitement.

Our society is still in infancy. Largely it supports the evolutionary possibility of human existence as the only legitimate way to be. Recent

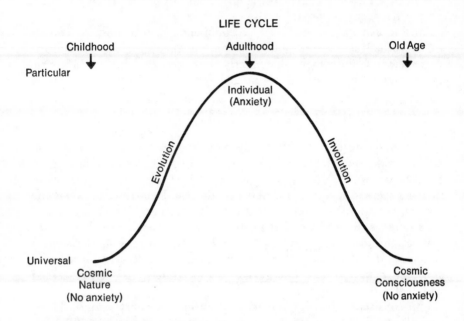

LIFE CYCLE

efforts of humanistically and existentially oriented thinkers and therapists have encouraged, with less than modest results, the adult stage of
existence as the paradigm for society. Still left out are old people.
Their eyes dim, their ears fail them, their bones weaken, their joints
ache, minds slow. Society does precious little to help these people to
understand that with the oncoming decay of the body there also ar-
rives increased opportunity for the release of the spirit. That may be
the finest hour—the summing up, the resolution—in our human existence.

Preparation for that insight must come early in life, in the evolutionary or adult period. When an old person needs philosophy it may be
too late to start teaching philosophy.

Index